Praise for
Getting It Done Right

Vincent Pettinelli's *Getting It Done Right: Pragmatic Wisdom for Human Service Managers* is a unique, insightful contribution to the field of human service management at just the right moment. He describes the elements required to offer people with disabilities superior care even when resources are scarce. Any leader/manager will benefit from his guidance because it is both accessible and useful.

Richard L Ludwick
President, University of St. Thomas-Houston

Reading Vincent Pettinelli's book was a surprising and eye-opening experience! Rather than theory, it provides a candid, almost casual, straight-talking narrative of insights and practical lessons from his own journey as a manager. In the process, he presents a diorama of his perspectives from the time he was a young, inexperienced manager to his thoughtful reflections as a seasoned CEO.

Pettinelli directs his comments to those who have risen (or are rising) through the ranks of an organization, offering insights on topics such as:
- The need for mentoring and peer support
- The importance of lifelong learning
- The conflicting demands of various funding entities
- The importance of being kind to yourself and others
- The value of professional trade associations.

This is a useful document for human service managers and

CEOs that will stimulate discussion and reflection on their own beliefs, attitudes and life goals.

Michelle R.B. Saddler
Former Secretary of the Illinois Department of Human Services

I am excited about the release of Vincent Pettinelli's *Getting It Done Right: Pragmatic Wisdom for Human Service Managers*. As Program Director of the MS in Human Services Management at National Louis University, I have selected it as one of the readings used in our Master's level gateway/introduction course, Human Service Management: Principles and Practices. As students begin the journey to enhance their leadership skills, this book offers an excellent and uniquely practical, comprehensive overview of the competencies a manager/leader will need to address the issues and challenges that inevitably arise.

The book is a quick read, written by, for and from a manager's perspective. You feel as if you are being personally mentored by the author. I would recommend that human service organizations get it into the hands of their managers at all levels. Readers may find it addresses many managerial situations/experiences they face and helps identify areas for further exploration and development.

Mark W. Doyle
Program Director, MS in Human Services Management
School of Health and Human Services
College of Professional Studies and Advancement (CPSA)

Vincent Pettinelli does an exceptional job of articulating the roles, responsibilities and rewards of not only being a good manager, but a great leader. His experience comes from years of work on the front lines. In addition, he makes it clear that building a great organization requires an investment in yourself and in your entire team.

Mark R. Klaus,
President & CEO, Home of Guiding Hands, El Cajon, CA

Getting It Done Right: Pragmatic Wisdom for Human Service Managers is an outstanding resource for those who aspire to leadership in human service organizations. Vincent Pettinelli provides a comprehensive look at the skill sets that leaders in this field need to possess and reminds them that success is achieved by delivering quality services to people with disabilities. The book will help students understand the unique needs of human service organizations and gain the skills to effectively drive positive changes in these organizations.

Beena George, Ph. D.
Dean, Cameron School of Business
University of St. Thomas-Houston

I wholeheartedly recommend *Getting It Done Right: Pragmatic Wisdom for Human Service Managers* by Vincent Pettinelli. As a member of his executive management team for 13 years, I had the benefit of observing his management insight and dynamic interpersonal skills in action on a daily basis.

This book details the management tools that Vince used so adroitly and honed for decades as an entrepreneur, enabling him to make VOCA one of the foremost success stories in the developmental disabilities field.

He artfully articulates how the effective manager must demonstrate the skills of a social worker who cements relationships and the talents of an entrepreneur who has vision and the fortitude to act upon that vision. Most important, he drives home the point that effective managers must be exemplars by "walking the talk"–being good listeners, celebrating staff, being responsive and assuring quality in their work. Thus their success does not rest solely on positional authority. It rests more on their personal power, a gift given by those with whom they work because they are viewed as capable, competent and caring managers.

Vince was indeed a mentor to all of us at VOCA, and he will mentor the readers of his book. I personally thank him for contributing to my ability to relate to others today both professionally and personally.

Thomas E. Pomeranz, Ed.D.
President and CEO of Universal LifeStiles, LLC

GETTING IT DONE RIGHT

GETTING IT
DONE
RIGHT

Pragmatic Wisdom for Human Service Managers

VINCENT D. PETTINELLI

High Tide Press

Published by High Tide Press
101 Hempstead Place, Suite 1A Joliet, IL 60433
www.hightidepress.com

Getting it done right : Pragmatic wisdom
for human service managers /
Vince Pettinelli

ISBN 978-1-892696-62-5

Printed in the United States of America

DEDICATION

This book is dedicated to my wife Judy.
For the past 44 years, she has stood by me
and my career, encouraging me to expand my
professional horizons.

Contents

Prologue   xiii

Introduction   xv

Chapter 1: Management as a Profession   **1**
Taking the Leap   1
Qualities of a Good Manager   6
Managing Risk   11
The Role of Managers in Human Service Agencies   14

Chapter 2: Organizing for Success   **17**
Quality Management   18
Managing Crisis and Change   25
Organizational Design   28

Chapter 3: Customer Satisfaction   **29**
Evaluating Service Outcomes   32
The Customers You Work With   36

Chapter 4: Coordinating Support Systems   **41**
Supervising Employees   41
The Organization Within the Organization   53
Advocates as Partners   60
Working with a Board of Directors   62
Change and Relationships   65

Chapter 5: Building a Solid Managerial Structure   **67**
Employee Recognition   67
Identifying Managerial Talent   69
Mentoring the New Manager   74
Training for Managers   77
Selecting Employees for Promotion   80
The Art of Delegation   84
Succession Planning   86

**Chapter 6: Managing Relationships
with External Organizations**   **91**
    Trade Organizations   91
    Consultants   96
    Unions   99
    Working with Government Officials   103
    The Publicly Funded System   107
    Lobbying   112
    Working with Bureaucracy   115

Chapter 7: Financial Considerations   **121**
    Financial Realities   121
    Becoming Proficient   125
    Structuring and Achieving Budget Goals   127
    Matching Client Needs to Available Funding   134
    Establishing and Maintaining Solid
    Banking Relationships   140
    Assets and Debt   143
    Measurement Makes a Difference   145
    The Politics of Reimbursement   148
    Fundraising in the Not-for-Profit Sector   152

Chapter 8: Making a Positive Community Impact   **157**
    Establishing and Enhancing Community Relationships   157
    Relating to the Media   161
    The Manager as Image-Maker   168
    Planning   169
    Marketing   172
    Selling   174

Chapter 9: Focus on Continuous Improvement   **177**
    Developing a Managerial Knowledge Base   181
    Giving Back   183
    A Sense of Balance   187

Epilogue   **191**

Appendix   **195**

Bibliography   **199**

About the Author   **203**

Prologue

It has been many years since the previously titled *Human Services Management That Works* was first published. The book was based on the growth and development of VOCA and its successor organization, PeopleServe. By the time we sold it, we were serving over 7,500 clients in 12 states, with 9,000 employees and an annual revenue of 350 million dollars.

In this second edition, my goal is to share some experiences and insights that I have had since that time. I believe the points I made initially still hold true for today's human service manager, in particular, that learning and practicing pragmatic skills that produce measurable results continue to be the most important function of a competent manager. I hope that what you read piques your interest and encourages you to grow into the best manager you can be.

This book is a collaborative effort with the staff and leadership of Trinity Services in Illinois, the staff and faculty at

National Louis University in Chicago and The University of St. Thomas in Houston.

Introduction

I started VOCA Corporation, an organization that serves people with disabilities, as a for-profit human service agency at a time when few such agencies existed because I was frustrated that even the best government agencies and not-for-profit organizations had almost no incentive for efficiency. It's not that the people who run private companies are better than those who run public agencies. It's that they survive for a very different reason. Government gets no kudos, no profit, no increase in business if it does its work well. In fact, the public doesn't even know if government agencies are working efficiently or not. Private business, on the other hand, functions in a competitive environment and will cease to exist if it doesn't make a return on its investment.

For example, at one point in my life, I became Commissioner for Mental Retardation** in the Pennsylvania Department of Public Welfare. I soon learned that the Office of Mental

---

*Today, the term "mental retardation" has been replaced with "developmental disabilities" or "intellectual disabilities."

Retardation* had paid private consultants $100,000 per plan for 12 strategic plans (completed over 12 successive years) to deinstitutionalize, modernize, save money, and generally improve the supports provided to the people receiving services. To make matters worse, my predecessor was in the middle of another contract to do yet another plan when I took over the job. I went ballistic. I said, "Is this why I'm here? Is my job to do perpetual planning or am I supposed to manage this operation?" On the other hand, I discovered a level of efficiency and responsiveness in the private sector I hadn't found in government. Now, a few years later, we are seeing an emphasis on more efficient delivery of services in the public sector–and not-for-profits as well.

To understand that evolution, we can take a brief look at the history of human services. Originally, government and small charitable organizations provided services for people in need or those cast off by society. It was thought that, since these organizations derived no profit, they obviously had a "mission" to work with the disenfranchised. In fact, "accountability" was determined by the willingness of agencies to serve people at very little or no cost. Officials and administrators perceived that to be enough.

Over the years, however, the number of people who need human service organizations has grown. Today's agencies find themselves confronted with an ever-growing population of people with life issues that are not easily remedied, ranging from developmental, psychological and physical challenges. Adding to the need, there has been a break-down in many of the social support systems, including family and religious organizations that cared for vulner-able people in the past. As a result, many people in distress find themselves looking for assistance from human service agencies. In this context, our job as human service admin-istrators is to serve these people by giving them the best shot at improving their quality of life in the best way we know how.

At the same time, we can't escape the economic perspective. Society says, "I care about homeless people and those with disabilities. But how much is my caring worth? One person needs a heart bypass but can't afford to pay for it. Someone else with a developmental disability needs a group home. A homeless person needs job training. Another person with an opioid addiction needs treatment. Everybody tells me there's not enough money to go around, so who's going to pay for all these needs?"

Clearly, as demographics change, more resources are needed. For instance, 50 years ago, many of the people we served would have died by the age of 50. Today, there are people in their 80s who will need support for the rest of their lives. Therefore, millions more dollars are now fun-neled into the technology of human survival, which has become one of the economy's fastest growing sectors.

Yet society does not know how to value such services. Many manufacturing jobs that previously provided substantial wages and stability have been replaced by service-oriented positions within human services and other fields that require more education and often offer lower salaries. Part of the problem arises from the difficulty of judging the efficacy of human services. If we're selling sugar, we can set our standards around unit sales. But when we sell human services, our standards are based on quality, not quantity. How do we quantify 50 pounds of quality human services?

That is why efficiency is so important. Those who provide services efficiently, who create measurable positive outcomes that can be seen, felt and heard, will not only get more done, they will be judged more favorably by society at large.

This shift may not be as dramatic as it would seem. As consumers, we often choose one product over another, not because it is substantially different from another similar product, but because it is marketed in a way that makes us want it more. The same is true of service delivery. A well-run agency concerns itself with the needs of individuals as well as with providing effective services at an efficient cost. While we may initially be attracted to a particular agency because of its philosophy of caring, we also must consider how efficiently and effectively that care can be provided. There isn't enough money to pay for everything at once, especially if we pay for it with our taxes. A human service agency can and will be held accountable in the same way as any other business if that agency hopes to survive in this new era of managed care, accountability and cost-efficiency.

Too often, human services has been a field where people hid from the accountability required by other industries. That is no longer possible as funders and clients demand that we be responsible stewards of public needs.

> **A well-run agency concerns itself with the needs of individuals as well as with providing effective services at an efficient cost.**

In the end, efficiency, good stewardship, good values and good management go hand in hand. That is why I am writing a book about management that recognizes it as a separate profession, as the point where accountability for service delivery takes form. Since many human service professionals aspire to management, I'll point out issues to consider from the time they are deciding whether to take a management position as well as the specialized situations they will encounter and must be prepared for when they take on the job.

For example, the best electrician, the one you want to rewire your house, can't just walk out of your living room into a new position as supervisor. Likewise, even the best clinician can't take on a new title and suddenly become an effective manager. Management is a separate profession that requires new skills.

I didn't know that when I made the transition, but I do now. In this book, I talk about the skills I needed to develop, and why. If you are at a point in your career where you are considering the transition to management, I hope that, as you continue reading, you'll think about the shifts you need to make when stepping from direct service into service management.

Management as a Profession

1

TAKING THE LEAP

The service manager at your favorite auto repair shop probably was at one time the shop's best mechanic. This former mechanic's only "qualification" for the management position was a good understanding of cars and how they work. Human services operate in exactly the same way; most of the managers have been promoted from the ranks of successful clinicians.

The assumption that a skillful mechanic or a skillful clinician will naturally make a skillful manager is a dangerous one. Mary Parker Follet, a social commentator in the early 20th century is often quoted as being the first to say that management "is the art of getting things done through people."[*] Today, the vision of a good manager incorporates that idea and goes beyond it. In the 21st century, good managers

[*]Sammi Caramela, "The Management Theory of Mary Parker Follett," (February 21, 2018). Retrieved from https://www.business.com/articles/management-theory-of-mary-parker-follett.

must know how to influence, listen and coach–not just give orders. They must understand and use technology and data. They must lead by example and represent the organization's values. And they must continually monitor and measure performance and systems against the goals of the agency or business.

A clinician, on the other hand, derives his satisfaction from the immediacy of client work. It can be excruciating for self-motivated clinicians to give up what they enjoy and are trained for, to leap into a job that is more removed from services provided directly to clients. But, if they aspire to management, they must make the leap.

If our mechanic loved to work with cars–absolutely loved it–he is going to hate being the shop manager. If he really relishes getting his hands greasy and tinkering with the engine to eliminate the noise that would never go away, perhaps he really belongs under the hood of a car. True, the shiny new title, the heftier paycheck, the office, the clean, well-pressed clothing, and the elevation over his former colleagues, are all very seductive. Yet the mechanic has to look past those lures and make a conscious decision: "Yes, I really can be more satisfied as the manager than I am as a mechanic."

How do you make that decision? One way is to make a list of the pros and cons of entering a new profession. Our mechanic could list what he likes and dislikes about working on cars and make a similar list of what the new job might entail. Conversations with an actual manager can confirm or change initial assumptions, especially if the mechanic asks whether he or she did a similar analysis before or after taking the job.

Let's say our mechanic decides to take that leap of faith. Those who do so quickly find themselves in a newly decorated office doubting the wisdom of their choice. The additional pay looks less attractive as they become alienated from the coworkers with whom they used to socialize, or when they find themselves having to defend the work that other people did.

If the mechanic is lucky, his boss will remember his or her climb up the supervisory ladder and coach him on what to expect. He or she might offer to talk and listen to what he is experiencing as a new manager or become his mentor.

Unfortunately, most appointing authorities don't do that–at least not automatically. So the first thing the new manager must do is make sure that training and mentorship will be available before taking the job. He needs to tell the service manager, "This is scary for me. When I become a foreman, you'll hire someone else for my position as mechanic. What if I can't make it? With 20 years experience as a mechanic and three months' experience as a supervisor, where am I supposed to go? I need your help."

Asking for help may encourage the boss to think that he or she is responsible for the newly promoted employee's success. And it will transform the relationship from one where the new manager is taking a leap of faith to one where he is making sure the leap is leading to solid ground.

The boss may think, "I'd better make sure this guy succeeds. If nothing else, he's a reflection of my judgment. If he does not work out, he can take down the rest of the shop even if things were going well before." So the decision to go from employee to manager is not as great a leap of faith as it would appear at first. It's in the mechanic's or the clinician's hands–to make sure the leap leads to solid ground.

The decision to go from employee to manager is not as great a leap of faith as it would appear at first.

If you're going to lead other people, part of that leap requires that you develop a relationship with those who are leading you. You need to know their mindset and be assured of their ability and willingness to support you. You need to be part of the system in a way you never were before.

Even with the best of preparation, and the best of mentors, some people never get past the feeling of abandoning their life's calling when they move to a position further removed from customers or clients. Supervisors who long to be doing hands-on work make bad managers. They need to prove to themselves and their employees how much better they are at a clinician's work, for example, than those who are actually doing it. Instead of guiding the hands of the people they supervise, they say, "Here, let me show you how it's done." In the process, they destroy the egos of their employees while stroking their own.

When you seek a job in management, you must commit yourself to learning a new professional discipline. A skilled chemist can't keep up-to-date on the latest advances in chemistry while managing 150 other chemists. Likewise, a psychologist who's learning new skills as a manager doesn't have the time to keep up-to-date on the latest best practices in clinical work.

You can't supervise while masquerading as SuperClinician. As you straddle the fence, you will lean further and further into the clinical side, which offers fewer risks and more immediate rewards than the management side. Both the organization and the people under you will suffer.

SuperClinician may not understand the problem. What's more, the administrator or supervisor who appoints the new manager often doesn't understand it either. He or she wants the agency's best psychologist to be head of psychology, thinking that if there's a problem, SuperClinician will be there to clean up the mess. What he or she doesn't think about are the skills needed to train and motivate others to do the job right. The appointing authority thinks only about the new manager's reputation for clinical excellence.

While new managers have to be aware of what's happening in the field to properly aid and supervise those under them, a new manager must commit to embracing a new profession and leaving the perspective of the single clinician. Certainly, the head of an agency concerned with addiction must know about the opioid epidemic, understand the spread of the disease and the responsibility of the serviced population to develop new behaviors. But that manager can't go to every seminar on every new treatment technology. That creates a false safety net of knowledge with no understanding of her newly chosen field–management.

QUALITIES OF A GOOD MANAGER

Working Through Others

As parents we take great pride in a child who brings home an excellent report card. In fact, our own work may be reflected in those good marks. Perhaps we drilled the child in math or offered research assistance on term papers. But we ignore our own participation and instead praise the child for his or her accomplishments.

In the same way, a good manager takes pride in the accomplishments of others without demanding personal recognition for the part he or she played in those undertakings. The manager gains fulfillment through the success of the organization and its staff. The best manager is one who can accept the criticism while giving away the glory. Yet few new to the job start out ready and willing to do that. It takes a maturing process.

> **The best manager is one who can accept the criticism while giving away the glory.**

A good manager soon finds out that managerial positions can be lonely. The support systems that existed for the clinician are no longer there now that the job has changed. Rewards come on a different level with every promotion.

My experience starting and building VOCA, a company that designed, developed and operated group homes for people with mental and developmental disabilities, showed how, as the business grew, my own work was farther and farther removed from the actual clients. When I began, I had one group home that served five people. I visited that home three times a day, was involved with nutrition programs, and personally helped bathe and dress the clients. I knew all the employees and their kids; they used to come to my house for dinner.

Then, I hired a supervisor with whom I worked while that person maintained the relationship with the employees and clients. Soon, I had three or four homes and had to hire supervisors to hire more supervisors. Eventually, I had 2,500 people in the organization serving 1,100 clients. My days were spent with contracts and comparing notes with other executives.

Our commitment to the client and to the value that the client's needs came before the company never changed. My personal commitment never changed. But I needed to change where I found satisfaction in my work from client interactions to the creation and maintenance of an organization that all those clients and employees would find dependable.

Professional Distance

Sometimes, maintaining professional distance requires hard choices. It can be difficult and even dangerous for managers to maintain friendships with colleagues who once worked beside them but now work under them. In fact, most managers, who have held supervisory positions for a while, will reluctantly admit they can no longer be friends with people they supervise. That doesn't mean they can no longer be friendly, courteous or responsive. But it does mean they can't expect people they supervise to be their confidantes. There are times when managers must have a level of detachment that enables them to look at what's best for the organization rather than what's best for an individual staff person.

This may be hard for human service clinicians, who are

trained to work with a wide variety of people. We human service workers have a tremendous need to be liked and feel included. It may be difficult for us, as we seek new spheres of support, to detach ourselves from the kinds of relationships we found so rewarding as clinicians.

So, if new managers, can no longer look to the old group for support, where can they find it? It is essential that managers network among themselves, sharing with one another either on an informal basis or through a well-thought-out supervisory structure that enables them to share their concerns in a private, safe, secure way.

Supporting Organizational Policies

A new manager has to learn a variety of new skills, many of which he or she never before considered important, such as mentoring, working with state government and understanding financial management. Each company also has its own rules and regulations. Managers are often surprised to find that they are more constrained at the supervisory level than they ever were as clinicians or other entry-level positions. If an agency or business is to thrive, it is up to management to work within and guard the organization's systems.

Good managers must be willing to take a stand and support an organizational policy whether or not it's a popular one. Often, they will have information unavailable to people at a lower level, such as knowledge of impending budget cuts. A manager must certainly advocate actively for as much funding as possible, but once a less-than-ideal decision is made, it is his or her responsibility to make the best of what's available and gain the fullest support possible from his or her subordinates.

This can sometimes mean working against personal beliefs. With legislation, court decisions and customs rapidly evolving on social issues, such as abortion, LGBT rights, women's rights, the role of religion and other issues, managers might find themselves in the position of needing to uphold a standard they might not have encountered before.

Managers must be willing to lay their professional and personal credibility on the line because many of the decisions they are forced to make will test their belief systems. At the supervisory level, a person no longer has the freedom to come across as reactive or to express personal preferences. He or she must be able to look inward and make adjustments necessary to live a style that is in everyone's best interest.

Remember that a manager represents the entire company or agency and its values, which might call for rethinking opinions in light of the best interests of the organization, its employees and the people it serves.

MANAGING RISK

The success of an agency or business depends on the per-formance of managers. Each manager becomes the face of success or failure to employees and clients even though he or she may have had little personal involvement in major decisions that affect the state of the organization. The actual decision-makers may be two or three echelons removed from the manager when, for instance, a board of directors holds ultimate responsibility. But he or she is the person that employees and clients alike look to as representing the company. It's a risky position to be in.

Managers must support the agency's objectives. Managers who find themselves in conflict with those objectives have two choices: convince the agency to change "its mind" or leave. A manager cannot and should not work against the organization's goals and continue in his or her position.

Integrity
Clinicians work with clients on a wide array of issues. To these clients, the clinicians hopefully represent a safe haven through which they may develop a new understanding of themselves, their skills and their abilities. To do that, clini-cians must maintain a high degree of integrity.

Managers must as well, and it isn't easy. Many people have an image of managers that is straight out of a Dilbert cartoon–the illogical, double-talking boss who creates uncertainty and anxiety. Add to this, that it is a natural tendency for people to resent those in control. Politicians are a good example. We elect them because we like what they stand for, but lose respect for them when they take office because, in our collective perception, we start to perceive them to be serving interests other than our own.

When a practitioner becomes a manager, there is a risk of being painted with that brush. Many new managers think they can lessen that risk by taking the title without taking on the responsibilities that go with it. They believe what their employees want is not a manager but rather someone who will facilitate and guide them as part of a democratic body to achieve what is in everybody's best interests. By teaming up with good people and having those people manage themselves, they think the best outcomes will be realized. In some cases, in fact, managers might even use this strategy to avoid being responsible for the results of their decisions.

That strategy will backfire. Employees lose respect for a supervisor who never makes a firm decision and never gives them the direction they need. And management loses respect for a supervisor who won't be accountable for the direction his or her employees are taking.

It's true that employee input and engagement are crucial. In fact, I say more about that below. But even the best employees need to know what outcomes are expected and the parameters of the system in which they work. That calls for hard decisions from management.

Along with the supervisory title come positional authority and personal risk. Successful managers can take that positional authority, incorporate it into their personal authority, and believe they truly serve the organization better from a position of leadership than as a member of the group. The catch? They have to enjoy leading more than following.

Somebody who hates to take charge of his or her own life, never wants to make a decision, and/or never wants to be accountable in personal relationships, is not a leader. That person will make a poor manager. A person who likes to lead is familiar with criticism for taking charge too quickly or trying to manipulate other people, and has borne the consequences. In spite of how others may react, a leader always goes back to that take-charge style.

So the risk goes beyond the job. It really is a risk of identity, of who you are. It's not an easy one to take. Before you embark on this new career, you need to find someone who can help you think through your willingness to take that risk so that when you find yourself being attacked, that person can help you understand your feelings. Why set yourself up like that? Because if you truly are a leader, you are driven to lead—so you do the best you can, and you deal with the pain.

THE ROLE OF MANAGERS IN A HUMAN SERVICE AGENCY

First-line supervisors often feel caught between higher level managers and clients. On one hand, they are advocating for the concerns of their clients and employees. But at the same time, they have to stay in line with the policies and interests of the company.

The best supervisors are the ones who know what they can change and what they can't, and agree to work within those parameters. They need to know where their levels of authority begin and end. They need to know when they can ask for help and when they should ask for help. They need to invite as much participation as possible from the people they supervise, recognizing that, after all their efforts to explain a particular policy, they will still have to demand compliance whether or not that policy is a popular one. That doesn't mean arbitrarily laying down the law; it means acting as a go-between, to check why employees or clients bristle at the policy and why it was instituted in the first place.

Some things will never change. Certain government policies, for example, may seem nonsensical to practitioners. Yet, as a supervisor, you have to enforce those policies or your agency will lose its funding. But other policies that seem equally ridiculous may be in place simply because no one ever questioned them. Don't make assumptions about which ones are which. Get the facts.

If you're like most people considering a first-line supervisor position, you are probably very young. This could be your first shot at management. You need a mentor, someone with whom you can share your feelings, and one whose understanding of the agency or company far surpasses your own. This is important, and I'm going to say more about it later.

But know this as you think about making the leap. If your supervisor is less capable than you are, you will learn nothing. Your decision to take that initial managerial position must depend in part on the availability of well-trained support from above. You need to know your supervisors bring an aura of experience that sheds light on the problems you are likely to face.

This will be true throughout your career. The old saying, "It's lonely at the top," is true. Top executives experience more risk than people at lower supervisory levels. People thrust into senior executive ranks unprepared will find themselves in a very lonely position because support systems thin out at the top. Typically, the only way left to find them is by networking with other high-level executives. That's where a board of directors can play an important role. The executive might identify one or two board members, the president, perhaps, or the chairperson, with whom to talk about ideas and values.

In addition, executives need a reliable subordinate with whom they can share feelings and concerns confidentially. Obviously, employees are sometimes reluctant to talk freely with superiors, but, without that window into the organization, executives risk being out-of-touch. However, I stress the word *confidentially* because, if that confidence is broken, irreparable harm is done.

Since companies thrive on new ideas, executives and supervisors alike must commit themselves to learning about new management ideas, technological innovations, and even procedures that have failed in other organizational systems. It's a serious mistake to think that those technologies, and the publications that discuss them, have no relevance to our industry. We are more like other businesses than we are unlike them. To claim that human services are unique is to ensure failure. It cuts you off from any meaningful learning experience you might gain from another industry. What's the difference between your agency and Starbucks or Amazon? From the standpoint of managing problems, nothing–both are concerned with the same issues: service delivery, fiscal constraints, public perception and quality.

Organizing for Success

2

Once you've set your sights on being a manager, you may find yourself looking at books and journals about management. You will probably notice references to different theories and practices with names like LEAN, SIX SIGMA, Agile, Kaizen, or other favorites of a particular author or consulting company. While the popularity and application of these models come in and out of fashion, and some methods may be best applied in manufacturing, health care, education or other fields, there are common themes and practices that are very relevant to human service organizations.

One methodology that I found very useful was Total Quality Management (TQM). TQM introduced the idea that organization-wide efforts could be put in place to create ongoing improvement in products and services. It was associated with the work of W. Edwards Deming, who helped recreate Japan's economy after World War II and then became a leading consultant in the U.S. Today, the strict model of TQM has evolved into a broader model of quality management, with concepts that are crucial for the new manager to understand.

QUALITY MANAGEMENT

As Aristotle noted, "Quality is not an act, it is a habit," and human service workers and managers must consciously develop quality habits. Steve Jobs encouraged Apple employees to "be a yardstick of quality," adding that "some people aren't used to an environment where excellence is expected."

Quality management is a cooperative form of doing business that relies on the talents and capabilities of both labor and management, working as a team to improve quality and productivity continually. One player can't do quality work without all the others, and quality work doesn't just happen because management wants it to. True quality is a result of people working together.

Developing Trust

Doing business cooperatively assumes that relationships between managers and the people they manage are built on trust. That trust in turn is built on the recognition by both parties that each has unique capabilities. Unless the groundwork is laid for that understanding, there will always be a separation of values, real or imagined, between the two groups. So building trust must be your first goal–and it takes a lot of practice.

At VOCA Corp., informal management/worker groups met continually to discuss ideas, plans and problem-solving opportunities. It came as no surprise when we started the system that each subgroup–managers and workers–was reluctant to share its pain, frustrations and concerns with the other. It is natural for people to maintain their beliefs and habits at the beginning of new situations. However, we found that a statement about how natural their skepticism is can clear the air, freeing the two sides to create bonds that might otherwise be more difficult to achieve.

It is, therefore, important to remember that if you communicate–even nonverbally–that "this is no place to talk about difficult issues," you'll never get off the ground. Trusting one another is what these groups are all about. If there were no trust issues, you wouldn't need committees to sit down and talk about feelings.

When managers work closely with subordinates, they are often taken aback at just how alienated employees can be. This is especially true in human service agencies because, since most of us have come up through the ranks, we pride ourselves on our ability to relate to other people. In fact, we may see ourselves as going out of our way to be accessible to staff. We probably believe we're coming across in a non-threatening manner.

So managers who aren't prepared for the initial skepticism of their working groups are in for a shock. They may react defensively, not understanding that this instinctive response can effectively kill any attempt at forming a meaningful working group.

To waylay negative reactions, quality efforts must start at the top and work their way down. It's up to the chief executive to behave in a way that will help other executives, subordinate-level managers, and employees feel comfortable about sharing their feelings and thoughts about the organization's culture.

What should managers expect from the early meetings? Complaints. Employees who have kept their fingers in the dike of gripes will now let out a torrent of complaints. Whether or not management sees those issues as valid, the employees who express them do. Management's receptivity to addressing the issues will set the tone for the work to come. And until the air is cleared, the real work of developing a quality organization cannot begin. Organizations that neglect this important starting point will fail to gain from efforts to promote quality.

Each person has his or her talents to add to the company's pool as needed. As managers and employees merge their talents, they will realize that the whole is better than any of the parts, that by putting their heads together they can drive the organization more effectively toward achieving high standards of quality and productivity. So the question becomes, what do quality and productivity really mean?

Cultivating Engagement

An organization must spend time assessing everyone's notions of quality standards to arrive at a collective definition that works. Everyone must be involved. No one, no matter how unrelated his or her task might seem, should be excluded; otherwise, the organization will quickly discover its efforts to implement quality services are being sabotaged by the very groups it has left out.

Collectively defining the company's quality standards and values is more difficult than it might seem. Typically, in human service agencies, the people with professional degrees do all the planning. But clerical workers, accountants and maintenance personnel, all have a role as important as that of the CEO in implementing the organizational quality standards. People live up to their expectations. When they are made to feel valueless, their behavior will match that perception.

An organization's quality standards depend on its collective self-identity. As people think individually about what quality means to them and how they can affect the organization's definition of quality, they develop a more personal commitment to the organization. At VOCA, when we went through the process, we had less employee turnover, fewer complaints and a decrease in behaviors that implied dis-satisfaction with the organization.

Chances are, the matrix on which your agency operates is not built on any standard of quality but rather on a hierarchical description of control. People understand their supervisory roles and the limits to their authority and responsibility. The traditional organizational matrix expresses the relative value of people in economic terms; that is, the people at the top of the company structure are worth more than the people at the bottom. Quality approaches say that everybody is valuable, we just do different things. Obviously, some of those things are a lot harder, a lot more risky, than others, but quality can work only if every individual is a contributor.

> **Quality can work only if every individual is a contributor.**

You can't direct someone to deliver quality. What you do instead is develop an understanding of the abilities that add to his or her growth and fulfillment as an individual performing a particular job. You help the individual redefine the concept of working and recognize the worth of his or her contribution. The person comes to believe that "I am more fulfilled, I am a better person because of the way I do my job than I would be if I were home collecting a monthly lottery check." This does not happen when the CEO pats maintenance workers on the head and says, "I know you just scrub the toilets, but we need you." The maintenance workers have to feel needed. It's much more difficult for the CEO to set up an environment in which a janitor feels valued than it is to walk into the restroom and say, "Thank you for the sparkling sinks."

So how does it happen? It happens when the CEO listens to that janitor in a way that communicates, "You really are important." It happens when everyone knows they are working in a culture where they are as eligible to hear a compliment and "thank you" as anyone else.

Perhaps you're a manager. Put yourself in that janitor's place. What do you want the CEO to tell you? You may want to hear, "We know you have lots of ideas you haven't told us about. And probably the reason you haven't told us is that you don't think we care about you or what you think. But you're keyed into the framework of this company in a way I as president never will be. You see it at its rawest, its most unabashed. You see people interact with one another. What's the tenor of what you hear? What do you think about how well people work together?"

Maintenance people are no different. They're invaluable. All of your employees are invaluable. So, when you evaluate how you're doing and how your employees are doing, make sure you get everybody involved.

Put yourself back in that janitor's shoes for a moment. You're probably going to be afraid that telling the CEO how you feel is going to cost more than you're willing to risk. You shouldn't. It's up to the CEO to create an environment in which you can express your ideas no matter how revolutionary they are, no matter how painful. Your ideas are worthy of toleration, if not always celebration.

As you discuss implementation of quality improvement, you will most likely see the need to redesign your reporting relationships. Work under the assumption that, rather than staying as it is now, your organization will change to better reflect what you want it to become.

For large organizations with scattered sites, communication among units poses one of the most severe threats to sharing ideas. You need to factor in extra time as you structure your planning groups. People in outlying areas, who may already feel alienated from the core organization, will need your help in understanding their responsibility to participate actively in the process. In order to feel invested in the new system, they will need representatives who have the power to channel discussions about the process as it happens. And if implementation of a quality approach is to take fire, you will have to check constantly on how well the most distant parts of the organization are responding.

One method is the creation of quality councils made up

of employees representative of various stakeholder groups throughout the company. These groups may discuss definitions and implementation of quality standards, and other matters. They can also provide feedback to ensure that management is on the right track. Management must, in turn, constantly acknowledge the councils, assuring members that their willingness to open themselves up to new ways of thinking, their unique and creative thought processes, are appreciated.

If you report to a board of directors, your board must also be involved in the process. Board members must be committed to the changes your agency will undergo if those changes are to have positive and lasting effects.

MANAGING CRISIS AND CHANGE

Take a look at the last major problem your organization faced. What happened? Who got involved in solving it? How many people knew about it? What rumors were started among the rank and file? How did you as a manager deal with those rumors?

Every organization has to deal with crises from time to time. They are a part of the growth process. How the organization handles crisis can be a true test of how well it has implemented quality systems and the organization's values.

Scapegoating, blaming and reactionary browbeating are indicators of a poorly developed organization that at best applies bandages to its wounds rather than giving them what they need to heal. Obviously, embracing a system that includes conversations, employee ownership of your mission, inclusion, and seeking better ways of going forward does not guarantee your agency a problem-free future. It does, however, promise that problems may be addressed in the most effective way possible.

The manner in which management responds to problems as they occur affects employees and clients. If you appear crisis-oriented, abruptly leaving meetings and constantly taking disruptive phone calls, the message that employees hear is that they are insignificant compared to the problem at hand. If, on the other hand, you attempt to deny that a problem exists, you are unfaithful to the commitment you've made

The manner in which management responds to problems as they occur affects employees and clients.

to developing total employee ownership of your company's mission. As awful as the problem may be, you're better off sharing it with everyone involved–you can't keep it secret for long anyway–so everyone can feel invested in its resolution. More than that, by sharing the problem, you help your employees understand why some parts of the organization might be preoccupied in resolving the issue. It might be difficult to share that information, but failing to develop a plan for the unexpected problems your agency will face is at best naive, at worst a cause for rapid deterioration of trust within the organization.

Many people in your agency may see the implementation of a quality program, with its emphasis on ownership, discussion and improvement, as a crisis in itself since it will, if effective, root out stubborn corners of resistance within the organization. People, who have performed their jobs the same way day in and day out for years unchallenged, will now be expected to change. Your personal enthusiasm for the process will not be shared by everyone. It will take longer than you think to get everybody to agree to the new language and concepts you espouse.

As your quality program is implemented, however, and as organizational changes occur, celebrate those changes as quickly as possible. You have three messages to deliver:

1. It's working.

2. It's a better way of doing business than we had in the past.

3. As painful as it may be, it's much better than the alternative of remaining dispassionate, unchanging and stunted in growth.

Your agency may be well-known, may have a long and glorious history, and may be at the forefront in providing services. That won't last unless you continually and forcefully meet new challenges. Sitting on your laurels makes you a stationary target.

ORGANIZATIONAL DESIGN

While people can be the strength of your organization, they can also be a source of organizational difficulties. Turning around a troubled business is usually dependent on executives and managers who are willing to change. This can be difficult and sometimes impossible, yet a major factor in a successful effort is how you've designed your organization.

Depending on the size and other characteristics of the company, some of the issues you might want to consider are the tasks at hand, how labor is divided, reporting relationships, who measures quality and what is measured, how sales expectations are set and met, and how inventory is controlled. Organizational design defines how the business is run and how people are served by an agency.

Customer Satisfaction

3

The concept of "customer" may be new for not-for-profit organizations since they generally don't perceive themselves as needing to sell anything to anybody. An agency's value, for instance, is not measured by the number of people it serves. Most of those people would not choose to be there because they would not choose to have the problem that requires that agency's services. How then is value measured? Management must set up criteria of excellence to measure the distance between what the organization says it is and what it really is.

I use the word "customer" to refer to the end users of the company's service systems. At first glance, that probably brings to mind the people who are actually served through the organization, that is, the clients. But for a quality approach to truly make a difference, you must attend to a number of stakeholders.

If your agency depends on state or federal money, you need

to demonstrate to government officials that you are indeed effective. If the funding office becomes dissatisfied for any reason, your funding will stop, and you will cease to exist. More traditional businesses also have pocketbook concerns, but in human services, where payments are often subsidized through third-party reimbursements, the payer base extends beyond our immediate understanding of who the client really is.

Other stakeholder-customers include state, county and federal agencies that support your services. And since many of the people our organizations serve are dependent on others to help them make decisions about their care, we must also include extended family members.

Then there is the public at large. In times like these, when money is becoming scarce, when people are extremely concerned about how their tax dollars are spent, the public is a critical customer base. How you are portrayed in the media, including social media, such as Facebook and Instagram, affects how the public–and your stakeholders–think of you.

Good relationships with news media, ranging from network to cable to key websites and print outlets, can help foster the general public's understanding of the value of your agency's services, especially if you rely on tax dollars for support. This is even more true of social media where, while good news travels fast, one misstep or perceived infraction can travel with lightning speed around the internet and even the world.

For example, early on, VOCA had some bad press about the kind of car I drove and where I lived. The assumption was that my car was too fancy to be supported by tax dollars. If people don't understand what you do and don't believe it has value, then whatever you do or wherever you live could be fodder for negative comments. There is less misperception about other institutions and executives. People don't care where Jeff Bezos or Elon Musk live. They are expected to live well. After all, they are CEOs of big companies.

Human services are, however, perceived differently. Even when tax dollars are not involved, there is often less perceived value, and people don't know how to determine when we're doing a good job.

Consequently, we need to explain to our media contacts and the general public how to evaluate our work. And we need to develop websites and a social media presence that explain what we do and why it is valuable. Sometimes this means sharing success stories as much as we can within the bounds of confidentiality. When we do good work, we need to let people know. This will add to the rewards we are able to reap. In addition, more people will join our ranks, and we will be able to do our work even better.

It's important that you take a broad view of your customer base, and include any and all constituencies that need to be involved in the process. How those constituencies evaluate your services will carry great weight in your own determination of how well your agency is performing its job. But regardless of all those other constituencies, the most important customers are still your clients.

EVALUATING SERVICE OUTCOMES

Human service professionals are wonderful at articulating axioms that border on the religious in their fervor: "We're here to serve people who have developmental challenges. We're here to serve the disadvantaged." What does that mean? Serve to do what? If an agency exists to provide services to people with disabilities so that they will no longer need those services, then one of the measures of success must be how many people have become more independent. How then do we measure that level of independence?

For a person with significant challenges, the measure might be the abilities to eat with a spoon and inform somebody that he needs to use the bathroom. Those are major achievements for someone whose IQ is less than 40. They mean that he can go with others to the movies or to a restaurant, that he has the social skills necessary for inclusion in a macro-social structure that up to that point had no use for him.

People with greater abilities might learn to be polite, be socially aware and use a bank account. They might even develop the skills to live independently. For that person, the avenues for inclusion can be substantially enhanced.

If we work with people who are excluded from society because they have a developmental disability or mental illness, our measure of success is how many of those people are more included than they were before. We cannot measure our success by the number of people who come through the door.

At VOCA we found it useful to think about how we should evaluate ourselves by identifying what our criteria would be and how we could show that we had met our own standards. As part of our self-analysis, I found it helpful to invite people to sit on our board who knew nothing about our business and ask their help in developing measures for us that made sense to them. Some very interesting ideas came out of those discussions, and most could be stated in plain language rather than resorting to professional jargon.

One of the measures of an agency's success must be how many people have become more independent.

Initially, our outside board members were unclear as to how they could be helpful. Knowing that they weren't psychotherapists or clinicians, they were reluctant to ask questions for fear of violating human service values and customs. But we wanted them to ask the questions we weren't going to hear from human service professionals. We wanted the questions their business sense was pushing them to ask–definable questions with definable answers.

I told them that nothing was sacred–a message I doubt they'd ever heard from most human service professionals. My experience with successful folks such as these is that when they need the services of mental health practitioners–perhaps marital problems or a son or daughter with developmental disabilities–they are extremely reluctant to seek help. Often that reticence is predicated on their lack of understanding of the process.

This gap in understanding may have surfaced when they needed some type of services for themselves or someone in their family. Perhaps they visited a human service professional, and started off by asking, "What are the outcomes of your services? Where are we going? What are we doing?" Clinicians are rarely able to articulate goals in a way that makes sense to people who think in quantitative terms.

When someone needs mental health counseling or has a family member with an intellectual disability, that person has to engage actively in the treatment process, commit to the process, trust the therapist, and understand the risks involved. Certainly, no clinician can guarantee results, but he or she must urge the customer to choose treatment based on some measurable outcome. As agencies disclose their methodologies in terms people can understand, their customers can make more informed decisions about whom to approach for help when they need it. You need to help people make better decisions about how they use the services offered.

We see this happening in other areas that years ago were more mysterious, such as pharmaceutical companies marketing to the general public for ailments ranging from diabetes to psoriasis. Once aware, consumers can decide if they want to discuss certain issues with their physician.

For example, in many situations, and depending on insurance plans, hospitals invite prospective parents to tour their obstetrical facilities. Does a woman prefer to give birth in a birthing room, surrounded by family and friends? Or is she more comfortable with the traditional setting, with only medical staff on hand? What type of anesthetic does she plan to have administered? Or will she choose to have natural childbirth? Once she knows her options, she can participate in making decisions about what is best for her.

So how do you help people participate in decisions about when to use your services? First, you need to know what you do. Evaluate your agency and ask these questions:

- ■ What makes us different from and/or better than our competitors?

- How do we continue to grow?
- What are our deficits, and how do we remedy them?

At the end of this assessment, you will provide better services than you did before. Clearly, you must be able to produce a measurable outcome. Simply caring about people is not enough. You must match your philosophy and commitment to quality care for everyone who comes to you with the reality of being able to deliver on that promise.

THE CUSTOMERS YOU WORK WITH

Another group of customers to consider are employees. Those who take ownership of the quality of services an agency or company provides will ensure that the recognized quality standards are implemented on a day-to-day basis. Conversely, employees who are unsure of how they fit into the organization or who think their values are different from the company's are a negative force. More often than not, they believe they're trying to do a good job in spite of the company's lack of support.

How do you know how your employees feel? You might look at certain macro indicators:

- Turnover rates
- The number of people with lengthy service records
- The number of involuntary terminations.

All are good initial indicators of how employees feel about your company. But no macro indicator takes the place of actually asking them to give you feedback.

At VOCA we used anonymous surveys as benchmarks to determine employee satisfaction. In the beginning, we were surprised at the detachment some of our employees claimed to feel from the company's missions and goals. What we found on further inspection was that they had created their own, frequently unrelated to the company's, when they didn't understand VOCA's goals. In most cases, once employees were able to verbalize the actual company goals and believed that the organization was verbalizing the goals and acting on them, they found they were closer to our mission than they had originally thought.

It's also a good idea to use employee focus groups, led by an experienced, outside consultant. If you really want employees to talk, you need to bring in someone who is not a part of your management structure. Regardless of how level your playing field, employees are likely to feel uncomfortable talking in front of you. They will feel free to express themselves only if the anonymity of their comments is sacred. This is the time to use outside help.

As you develop an atmosphere of trust, you will find people willing to open up more and more often. But they' ll never tell you everything you want to know. You must continue to provide safe ways for people to give their feedback on how you're doing. Assume that what they're telling you is not because they want to hurt you, but steel yourself for what you're going to hear.

In articulating the agency's mission, you will weed out perennially disgruntled employees. People, who on the surface may appear to be dedicated, stick out like sore thumbs when that dedication fails to meet the implementation test. Caring about people is not enough. You and your people must act as if you care.

In the human service field, we are besieged with philosophers who have trouble dirtying their hands or who have been out of the trenches so long they've forgotten what it was like to actually own and implement services. In our company, we found such people rely heavily on techniques they used many years ago, assuming them to be applicable to what clients need today. They held on to their old ways of doing things because it was comfortable for them. By continually redefining an agency's quality standards, you help employees develop new and meaningful commitments to serving clients in ways that are most beneficial to each individual.

> **As you develop an atmosphere of trust, you will find people willing to open up more and more often.**

One of the ways we at VOCA said, "We appreciate you," to

our employees was by paying them what we (the company)–and they–thought they deserved. Pay scales are often set up with no acknowledgment of what an employee needs to make a living wage. Somehow, employers expect that salary structures set up 20 years ago should be applicable to today's market. In human services, we are very good at saying, "This is all we have to spend."

Wage issues will confront you as a manager since you must balance what your employees need with the knowledge that, unfair though it may be, higher wages dependent on tax dollars are not popular with the public. In fact, they may actually diminish public support for your agency.

Still, if your agency is supported by tax dollars or other contributions, you can sometimes challenge your level of support effectively. At a minimum, you need to look at other agencies and similar jobs in other businesses to gather data on what reasonable compensation and benefits plans should be for people at all levels within your company. This will allow you to create a compensation scale that fosters employee dignity and respect that you can present to your funders. By failing to review and measure your compensation plans periodically against those in the business community at large, you continue to depress the reality of what it costs to provide quality services.

I was trained as a social worker, a profession started by

women in urban areas, who could afford to work with the poor and receive no compensation. This was at a time when one income families were common, and women did not have to worry about supporting their families.

More than 100 years later, it is still difficult to articulate the need for reasonable pay for an occupation founded on that level of volunteerism. But, because of human service professionals, there are lots of people better off today than they ever were before. What value does society place on that? How much is it worth? We have to start telling people we deserve a living wage.

At VOCA we turned down many new business opportunities when funding agencies were unwilling to recognize the needs of our employees. Rather than pay people too little to keep them invested in their jobs and their mission, we elected not to take on new contracts whose reimbursement was insufficient to fund a quality level of service.

With cutbacks in available dollars, budgetary realities are forcing us to demand that funding agencies take a close look at our situation. The quality of services becomes depressed beyond minimally accepted standards when we are unable to hire the best people to perform needed services. It's a continuing fight in the field of human services. We cannot take it quietly.

Coordinating
Support Systems

4

SUPERVISING EMPLOYEES

There are many definitions of "supervisor" ranging from the perfunctory "one who supervises," to more complex statements reflective of different aspects of management. Consultant and author Carter McNamara adds that "supervisors are typically responsible for their direct reports' progress and productivity in the workplace."[*]

I define supervision as an understandable, mutually agreeable conduit of behavior through which employees can realize both the company's objectives and their own. That definition states in essence that a manager can only supervise someone who knows his or her job, acknowledges that it can be done more readily with the manager's help, and actively decides to do it. The manager, in turn, must be will-

---

[*]Carter McNamara, "A Definition of Supervisor," Blog: Supervision (March 20, 2011). Retrieved from https://managementhelp.org/blogs/supervision/2011/03/20/a-definition-of-supervision.

ing to help employees define aspects of their responsibilities that may augment what is in their job descriptions and help them over any hurdles that may occur. In other words, the supervisor and the employees must develop a contractual relationship, informal though it may be.

In addition, the supervisor must understand the employee's job completely. The employee, in turn, must understand the supervisor's job, at least as it relates to his or her own position. The two must act, in effect, like partners. Supervisor-partners must be able to describe in as much detail as necessary what the job entails–the time and skills it requires as well as the type of work involved–and be responsible for creating an environment within which the employee-partner relationship may develop and grow. They must take into account the special talents the employee brings to the job and allow that person to flesh out the responsibilities in a way that reflects his or her expertise.

The key here is not to force the person to fit the job description. Every job naturally has its own duties, and whoever takes it must perform them. That person needs baseline skills and a certain educational background. But beyond that, what makes work enjoyable is the person's ability to make an imprint on the job, to own it. Of course, it is rare to find an employee 100 percent suited for any position. The supervisory relationship must include a decision between the two partners to use the assets the employee brings to the job and actively plan to remediate as many of the deficits as possible. The time to initiate the planning is at the beginning of the relationship, not a year down the road during a performance evaluation.

In addition, it is the manager's responsibility to shape an environment that fosters individual growth and creativity. That means getting to know the employee as a person, not just as a body occupying a spot somewhere along the chain of command.

Ideally, the two partners sit down and talk, assessing the employee's skills, strengths and deficits as they pertain to the job. That's hard to do during a job interview because the prospective employee always wants to put his or her best foot forward. But my experience has been that candidates willing to do such an assessment tend to be more successful in finding jobs. Every supervisor knows there is no perfect applicant–nor, for that matter, a perfect supervisor. The objective is to work out the best arrangement possible, given both partners' foibles, so that each knows going into the deal what the other's strengths, weaknesses and idiosyncrasies are.

That means the supervisors must also be willing to share such information. "I know there are things that make you angry," they might say, "but I don't know what they are. Would you talk to me about some of those things? What might I do inadvertently that would make you angry?" And they must also say, "I'm glad you told me that because I have this sensitivity about...."

That begins a relationship. But it takes two people who can sit down and have an honest, adult conversation. It may be a long, tedious task for the supervisor to get the employee to the point of feeling comfortable enough to engage in such a discussion, but all supervisory relationships must work toward that end.

Managers who can't free themselves from the day-to-day operations, who have never made the leap from SuperClinician to manager, don't have the time to cultivate relationships with their employees. If you're busy from the moment you walk into the office each morning until the moment you leave, you're doing your employees a great disservice. If you want to get to know them better, take time to walk around and say, "How are you?" Have a cup of coffee with someone. Drop by an employee's office. You can learn a lot that way, but it means putting unstructured time into your schedule.

In addition, a successful supervisory relationship hinges on feedback. If an employee has to wait for an annual evaluation to know how well he or she is performing, something is very wrong. Feedback must be constant. When supervising people, they should be able to tell you, the supervisor, how well they're doing at any given moment of the day and know that you too are aware of how well they're doing. You should be telling them enough about their performance that there's no question. I'm always chagrined at the response some people give when told they're not performing up to par. "But I'm working 14 hours a day!" they exclaim. Their message? Hours of work equals efficacy of work. That is simply not true.

Conversely, you should be aware of how well you're doing as a supervisor. Although that sounds easy, it's obviously very difficult. But if you can set up a culture of employee trust, an atmosphere of openness rather than intimidation, and give employees a vehicle to reflect back

If you can set up an atmosphere of openness rather than intimidation, employees will feel comfortable about offering their honest opinions.

their perceptions of how well you're managing the organization, they will feel comfortable about offering their honest opinions when needed.

Of course, you must realize that when you offer feedback, you always run the risk of offending someone. However, if you don't tell that person, you'll likely offend him even more because he'll sense that something is wrong.

An old Italian proverb states, "Never let the sun set on an argument." It's good advice. If you can't get your feelings out, they seethe, corrode and corrupt relationships. It takes a lot of guts to open up. You're going to misperceive and you're going to misinterpret, so just say, "I'm sorry." It's that simple. At least you've tried, and you've delivered the most important message–you care. You can't lose with that.

Performance Appraisal

Unexpected moments of reinforcement are great for building relationships. An annual evaluation, on the other hand, tends to be stilted and defensive, something both supervisor and employee want to get out of the way as quickly as possible. Still, the process offers valuable evidence that the relationship is as it should be, and it's an important document if there should ever be a major dispute between the agency or company and an employee.

I chose to give evaluation sheets to my employees and ask them to rate themselves. My assumption was that if an employee can't evaluate himself honestly–or worse, if his evaluation of himself is substantially different from my own–we have a major communication problem. The evaluation is a good diagnostic of the efficacy of our partnership.

The review also provides documentation of areas the employee needs to work on and what the supervisor can do to enhance the employee's performance. What are a supervisor's responsibilities, for example, if an employee needs to learn fiscal management skills? If fiscal management is an essential part of the job and the supervisor is unwilling to see that the employee is given the money and the time to attend seminars, the supervisor effectively makes it difficult or impossible for the employee to develop that skill. The employee knows he or she cannot be successful in the job and must either choose to leave or be fired.

Ideally, the annual evaluation is a reaffirmation of the relationship. Of course, there are employees who need that piece of paper in their hands, especially if they're unsure of themselves or new in the company. They may even need more regular written evaluations. The "annual" review might actually occur two or three times a year–whatever is appropriate for the organization.

The format of the written evaluation also needs to be flexible. For upper-level employees, narratives about the job and the relationship tend to be more useful than checklists. A checklist, on the other hand, seems to work better for employees who are in more direct ranks of service, who need more tangible feedback. It's a less-than-perfect quantitative measure of qualitative attributes, but it's the best we have.

Evaluations are also a wonderful tool for a higher-level manager to get a bird's-eye view of how a subordinate manager operates and what he or she perceives as important. The comments employees write on the evaluations, the number of employees who refuse to sign them or who reject them as unfair are good indicators of the relationships a supervisor has with his or her employees. By reading between the lines, the upper-level manager can often derive a realistic view of how well that supervisor is doing.

Enhancing Employee Involvement and Motivation

Most employees want to be involved in the company. And most are at their motivational peak the day they're hired. The time to begin engaging and inspiring an employee is the day he or she walks in the door, before the informal network steps in, and malcontents say, "Oh, this is a terrible place, terrible; watch out for the boss." During orientation, give new employees a hook into the organization, even if they know very little about what they're to do. Celebrate the addition of the new employee's skills, talent, and time to the agency. In business, we always give going away parties but rarely give coming-to-work parties. We need to give more coming-to-work parties.

> **We need to give more coming-to-work parties.**

New employees' perceptions of what your company or agency does are probably 35 to 40 percent off, even though they have gone through job interviews. Their success in the company depends on their getting in sync with the reality of what you do. You can help paint a realistic picture of the environment and work expectations, including the pace, goals and daily responsibilities.

Make frequent rhythm checks on new employees to make

sure they are dancing in step with everyone else. The worst thing that can happen is for an employee to start improvising her own steps and come out of her office to find everyone else is doing a lively rumba. Suddenly, that employee doesn't want to dance anymore. She's afraid. Rather than dance the wrong steps again, she won't dance until she learns the steps everyone else is doing.

As a supervisor, you need to help the new employee hear the music the others are dancing to. One way of doing that is to have the new person spend time with peers you would like her to emulate or suggest that she join them for coffee breaks or lunch. It's easier to learn the dance steps in small, informal groups than it is sitting alone and reading dance notations. The agency needs to have a policy that employee involvement is not only appreciated but expected. The message must truly be, "We can't run this place without you."

How that actually works within the company must be well thought out. The test for the employee is his or her relationship to its mission and the expectations. Answering the following questions might help develop positive rapport:

- How does my job contribute?
- How do I contribute?
- Does the company really care what I think?
- How does change take place here? Is it always from the top down?

- Is my input solicited?
- What's happened to other people here who have made suggestions? Have they been rewarded?
- Do I receive incentive pay for performance, for new ideas?
- Are people with new ideas cherished and developed, or are they pushed aside?

Let's consider a maintenance worker, who, after fixing the same faucet half a dozen times, decides that a new valve would solve the problem once and for all. The faucet was put in during recent, costly renovations and the valve will take another $200 out of your dwindling budget, but the maintenance worker estimates it will save the company $700 in repairs over the next several years. Should he take that information to a supervisor who's strapped for cash? He will if that supervisor is willing to listen to his explanation of the problem. What might at first sound like bad news is in fact a positive statement of employee involvement.

In addition, the supportive manager learns not only of a long-term cost saving idea but also, perhaps, of a skill he wasn't aware the maintenance worker had. The maintenance worker has performed his job in a way no one had anticipated, and both he and the manager should celebrate this creativity. It doesn't take a graduate degree to show that level of creativity. The truth is that everyone wants to take pride in his or her work. Quality, then, is redefined by the relationship between the supervisor and the employee.

Then again, maybe the manager had at least a hint of what to expect from this maintenance worker based on initial interviews. When interviewing a job candidate, you can gather these hints by looking for more than simply whether the person can meet the requirements of the job description. Ask yourself, "Would this person be able to develop the job into more than I now intend it to be? Can we, because we click, develop a supportive, trusting relationship? Because if we can, I don't have to worry that this person will feel awkward telling me his or her feelings, and I don't have to watch my word choices either." This perspective alters the supervisory process so that it becomes more about the relationship.

We currently see more and more companies taking the idea of building such relationships to heart. We see it in the open floor plans in office environments that foster communication between workers and supervisors. We see it in management training courses that stress coaching, dialogue and the importance of listening to front-line workers. We see it in the invitations that tech and other start-ups offer employees to share in rewards as the company succeeds, and we see it in the growing awareness that recognition and support can actually be as important as those dollars in retaining and motivating employees. The message to employees? "We want you to succeed here. We will support each other."

That was a new idea for us at VOCA since we had started off working in the old, paternalistic tradition. Because some of us had graduate educations and some of us didn't, it was easy for those of us with letters after our names to say, "You must not be as creative and bright as I am. Look at me. I have a degree. I have a diploma hanging on my wall."

What made the difference for us was the kind of employees who, even though they didn't have degrees, had the gumption to say, "Listen to me. I really do have good ideas." That was years ago, but I can still name those folks. It was a revelation to me. I thought, "If there are two or three employees like that, are there 500? Are there 1,000? Can I expect this of all my employees? If not, what does that say about them, about us and about their fit within this organization? What does it say about our selection criteria?"

It catalyzed my decision to rethink how we employ people. We grew so quickly in the beginning that a lot of times we hired people simply to fill jobs that needed filling. One year we grew by 35 percent and hired 400 people. You can't hire 400 people in just a few months and have a mutually enriching atmosphere. You have to spend time with people to develop it.

THE ORGANIZATION WITHIN THE ORGANIZATION

One thing to keep in mind when you become a manager at whatever level is the likely presence of an informal organization within your formal structure. In a larger company, the informal organization is divided into subsets, such as the support staff, the subordinate management staff, the technicians, IT, the accountants, etc. And the subsets are not tightly sealed; there's bleed-over between them. You may experience this as an "invisible force" that can work for or against your efforts at alignment and communication. In a healthy company, the informal organization involves positive people who are aligned with the formal organization's goals and will serve to reinforce those goals. In a dysfunctional company, the power brokers of the informal organization are negative people, the naysayers who will have the opposite effect.

Once an employee ascertains what the formal organization says on any given subject, what will he or she hear from the informal network of conversations and social media contact between employees? Most often, the organization's message and the informal network will not say the same thing.

Supervisors who ignore this network will not succeed. Instead, they should know how the network can be helpful since there is often truth in the grapevine. Employees are often more likely to trust what they hear from coworkers than what they hear or read in "official" communications. Managers need to listen for and evaluate these informal messages because they do exist. Anyone naive enough to say, "This doesn't happen in my company," will be proven wrong.

As a manager, you probably will not hear these messages directly, but you need to know what they are. The only way you can do that is to have people you trust who can tell you what they're hearing. These people need to know they will not be chastised or exposed for telling you what you need to know to help make the organization better. You need people who know you for what you are and who haven't painted you as an "enemy" to be avoided.

Sometimes you might be able to go back to the people you used to socialize with before you became a manager, although the relationship will no longer be the same. Once you identify and talk with those who will be your network, the relationships with them border on sacred. If you violate the relationships, you will make enemies for life and your credibility will be gone. The key is to be ethical. If you single people out to solicit confidential information, then you are putting them in the position of corporate snitches. But a skilled manager should be able to elicit perceptions of how smoothly the corporate or unit wheels are turning in conversing with employees. It takes sensitivity, a good ear, and a willingness to ask people how they're doing and listen to their answers.

Am I talking about a corporate spy ring? Not at all. Every organization depends on the transmission of information. In an ideal world, we wouldn't need to look behind the scenes; the word within the formal and informal organizations would be the same. But it just doesn't work that way. And it's important that, as a manager, you are in the know.

The informal organization feeds on rumor. Therefore, the best thing a company can do once it has made a decision that affects its workforce is tell the employees immediately, even if the decision is painful. Trying to keep it under wraps is impossible; it will leak out. (The size of the organization, by the way, has nothing to do with the spread of information.) And if the informal organization gets access to the information months before the decision is announced, it will accumulate power beyond belief. Often a company not ready to make an announcement will have to do so because the rumor mill demands it. The informal organization pushes the formal organization to bend to its demands. In fact, the announcement may cause an explosion like an atomic bomb, and the managers involved may never be the same. It's devastating.

There are varying degrees of meshing between the formal and informal organizations, but the more the two are out of sync, the more pathological the effect. If the informal organization sends out negative information that the company is facing distressing or tragic circumstances while the formal one keeps celebrating how wonderful the company is, something is very wrong. The organization is not aligned.

Leaders of the informal organization have a tremendous amount of power. In an ailing agency, the leaders may be people who have very little actual positional power but who thrive on the dissatisfaction of others. They take the smallest problem, blow it up as large as possible, and lead the chant about what a terrible place they work in. If the formal organization does not see that happening and establishes new changes in policies and/or procedures, the malevolent informal organization will make sure the changes fail.

In that case, the organization is due for some serious conversations. And the managers will want those conversations because they are the ones employees hold responsible. As a result, they feel as if they were wearing a sign that says, "If you're feeling bad, kick me!"

You have to make changes when necessary, even if the task is difficult. In fact, if you are in a situation without the power to make changes, you may be in the wrong place. If you sense that you will likely be in a powerless position before you take the job, you may not want to take it in the first place.

However, there are frequently workable solutions if you are willing to listen to people and make adjustments. Talk with them about their perceptions of the identified problem and see if you can reach agreements about what is needed to resolve it. When you interact with people like this, they are usually more willing to change, and you might discover changes that you need to make as well. Accomplishing this requires a comfortable employee environment where people are encouraged to participate in the process. Yes, that can be tough, especially if the bad feelings precede your arrival on the job. So it is wise to find out what is causing the negativity.

When people tell you, "I hate my job," you can respond with, "I hate my job, too–sometimes." Then ask them, "What do you hate about your job?" The reply you want to hear is one that begins with, "I hate it when...." You need specificity. People who say, "Well, I don't know, I just hate it," have no genuine argument against you, or company policies and procedures. But if there's a significant group of malcontents, there is a reason for that dissatisfaction, and you need to find out what it is. Then you need to work with your employees to resolve the issue.

Just stating the issues often does a lot to relieve them. For instance, "I don't understand why we don't have Diet Coke in the pop machine," can be solved easily. On the other hand, "I don't understand why some people here got a 10 percent pay raise and our division didn't get anything," can begin a good discussion.

A problem we had at VOCA years ago was, "My schedule changes constantly. I can never predict time off." We had people working 24 hours a day, 365 days a year. Certain employees had Wednesdays and Thursdays off while other employees consistently called in needing to take Wednesday and Thursday off. Having only so many people to pull from, a supervisor would have to go back to the employees scheduled to be off and ask, "Can you come in?" Most people didn't mind that occasionally, but when it happened over and over, they started thinking, "This organization doesn't care about us. We're just functionaries."

Our managers had to fix that. If they allowed some employees to take off willy-nilly without corrective action, other employees, who always showed up as scheduled, ended up paying the price. As long as the managers treated people simply as bodies needed to fill slots, employees didn't care if the program lived or died.

The problem was solved after managers developed appropriate schedules and impressed upon employees the importance of showing up for their appointed shifts. Dedicated employees were no longer deprived of their days off at the last minute to work overtime, and were assured that they did in fact deserve that time off and should have it. Employees who were abusing the system were let go. We also found part-time people who loved filling in. The part-time employees who really were good became full-time employees.

What causes chronic absenteeism? You won't know unless you ask. Sit down with the offending employees and ask, "Do you know what happens when you take off?" You might hear, "No, I never thought about it." But you might also hear, "I've had a lot of doctors' appointments. I have cancer."

> **If you create a comfortable environment for employees within a positive culture, you'll be surprised at how many seemingly unhappy employees will begin to thrive.**

If you create a comfortable environment for employees within a positive culture, you'll be surprised at how many seemingly unhappy employees will begin to thrive. But some you won't reclaim, especially if their real motivation and satisfaction came from being disruptive or vindictive. If they don't develop more positive attitudes, they have to be ferreted out. And the message to other employees has to be, "Because we care so much about what we're doing here, we won't put up with somebody who is that malevolent." Maybe those people can change somewhere else.

At VOCA we developed organizational diagnostics as an effective way to look at measurement and help managers put their fingers on the pulse of the company. Today, there are many such diagnostic tools that utilize surveys and take the "pulse" of an organization. Such survey tools have been statistically validated, and they help make attitudes and cultural norms visible to everyone in the company. Frequently, when everyone can look at a report and see how their organization appears, ensuing discussions can surface issues and help solve them. An example of VOCA's goals and accompanying questionnaire for employees appear in the Appendix.

ADVOCATES AS PARTNERS

In human services, we get feedback from any number of sources–our clients, certainly, but also courts, court-appointed guardians, and a myriad self-appointed advocacy groups. There are also numerous advocacy organizations, including state and local ARC's, concerned with the full inclusion of people with disabilities in society. Another force that has emerged is the presence of self-advocates, who may work primarily with the people your organization serves. These outside groups take it upon themselves to ensure not only that the services we provide are good for the people who are receiving them, but also that the services are being delivered well. They look beyond government regulations.

Many providers consider their relationship with advocates to be adversarial. They always have something to say although they are not in the thick of things as we are. For instance, they typically are not cognizant of the trials and tribulations of service delivery, be they funding problems, personnel problems, or other issues. However, we should see advocates as partners in achieving what's best for our clients. If an advocate doesn't understand the workings of a particular delivery service model, system or result, we either need to improve what we are doing or improve how we describe it.

Advocates should recognize the organization's values and be committed to serving them. Additionally, they need to be able to understand the support and services that are very personal, and see the connection between needs, wants and outcome achievement. Conversely, the organization should ensure that its person-centered services are genuine, valued by the person being served and reflect changes as goals evolve. As mentioned previously, strong data management and a strong culture enhance the advocacy partnership.

A lot depends on the advocate's perception of a particular agency's mission. If advocates see an agency working with people who are depressed and those people are not getting better, then they may need more detailed information about the complexities of particular cases. However, we must work with advocates to set realistic expectations. If the advocate expects that everyone with an addiction is going to be cured, and they judge an agency by that standard, then everyone loses.

A better way to relate to advocates involves forming a partnership early on. Develop an understanding, welcome that third-party review, and work together to establish criteria that meet everybody's needs. That technique can work with any potentially adversarial group or individual.

WORKING WITH A BOARD OF DIRECTORS

The boards of directors of most not-for-profit human service agencies are usually drawn from people in the community. There may be businesspeople, especially donors and/or people who feel a connection to the client population; parents of people in the client population; and prominent citizens who may sit on the boards of several agencies.

The executive director finds him or herself responsible to this board of directors, many of whom have limited knowledge of what is happening day-to-day in the organization even though they receive financial statements each month, come together to see presentations and often vote. But the truth is, unlike a proprietary board of directors, a not-for-profit board rarely runs or sets policies for the agency. Board members sometimes act as rubber stamps for policy changes the executive director recommends.

That works well until a problem arises. If a disgruntled employee writes directly to the board or if there's a problem with service delivery, a lawsuit or some other crisis, the board members may get "mean." They feel guilty about their lack of involvement. Their integrity is now called into question because their names are associated with an agency that's in trouble. Suddenly, they are very concerned, and the person who takes it on the chin every time is the executive director as he or she faces questions, such as "Why didn't you tell us? It was your responsibility. When we approved this, we thought...."

So it is wise to establish prerequisites for those interested in serving on the board. Require that your members take ownership for their service. If they don't have the time, they shouldn't serve. It's ludicrous to have titled members of the community just so you can say your board consists of all these big shots. Rather, have unknown people who have the time to get involved and understand how your policies work, not so they can make changes, but so they can understand how you provide services to people. They need to see all the pimples and scars, and all the things dollars can and can't provide. They need to know what's going on so that when you are attacked–and you will be–they can rally behind you.

Not-for-profit board members sometimes seem to check their common sense and business sense at the door when they deal with a human service agency. They have the notion that, because we work with people who have various disabilities, all the things that work for people in the "real" business world don't apply. It is the director's job to help the board understand the agency and the population it serves. If board members become actively involved in a qualitative and quantitative analysis of the agency's services, if they understand what the agency does, they are less likely to act as a rubber stamp. In addition, not-for-profit directors and their boards need to look at what they're doing through proprietary glasses and ask some hard questions: "Is what we are doing worth buying? Is it meaningful?" The bottom line numbers in proprietary companies answer those questions.

> Not-for-profit sometimes seems to connote "not serious." That's dangerous. If a not-for-profit agency doesn't have retained earnings, if it isn't bringing in more than it spends, it's going to go out of business just as quickly as a proprietary company will.

Sometimes entrepreneurial private companies hesitate to invite outside directors to join because they don't want interference. That's what we did at VOCA–at first. In the beginning, VOCA's board was made up of our internal executives. I didn't want to take the risk of letting some board of directors make a decision–VOCA was everything I had.

As I became more comfortable with what we were doing and more willing to expose myself, and developed good relationships with people I trusted, we included outside directors, people who had made their marks and were now ready to help someone else out. They were not rubber stamps, and they clearly added views on the efficacy of what we did that our inside people couldn't. I came to understand that an outside perspective can help. On the other hand, they had less at stake. They didn't work at VOCA; they didn't have to wear the results of what we did every day. They could afford to urge action that we might, at first hearing, have considered too risky.

CHANGE AND RELATIONSHIPS

When an executive director leaves after 10 or 20 years, the next person in line is in trouble. Typically, long-term directors have developed not only professional relationships with board members but personal ones as well. Board members don't know how to work with the new person in a pinch. "I knew Bob," they say. "I don't know Barbara. If Bob were here, this wouldn't have happened."

New directors need to be very careful in taking over an agency that has had stable leadership for a long time. If they don't convince the board to realize that they are not "Bob" and internalize what that means, they cannot be successful.

If you are the prospective director, you need to consider the situation carefully. At the time of your interview, the board will ask questions and then ask for questions from you. That's the time to say, "You had 20 years with Bob. I'm going to be new. How do I know that I'm going to get a fair shot? What kind of support can I count on?" That should open a discussion about the relationship the board wants with a new director. Don't take a job without that understanding. If the board is not willing to support you, you have nothing to fall back on.

If you do take the job, you need to work at developing relationships as quickly as you can with as many board members as possible–try for a majority. Certainly, you need the chairperson on your side. In a not-for-profit agency in particular, the chairperson is your champion when the executive committee meets without staff.

Maybe the board members have continued to serve because they liked the executive director, not because of their interest in the agency. In that case, it might be time for them to leave when the director does. It's okay to say that. It needs to be worked out ahead of time with the board chairperson, who can be the prime mover in assisting you with recomposition of the board. If, on the other hand, board members can see beyond the new director's personality to the mission of the agency, that director can provide a new look, a different way of providing services. The new director's way is neither better nor worse, just different.

Building a Solid Managerial Structure

5

EMPLOYEE RECOGNITION

Early in its development, VOCA had 2,500 employees in six states. Wanting to meet as many of them as possible, I'd made it a point to travel to each of our locations. At each visit, I stayed two or three days and had a town meeting with the employees. I invited them to share their concerns in a community setting and let them know that VOCA worked as a community effort. Before each of those meetings, I met with managers to find out what they perceived as issues for their employees. During the meetings, employees had an opportunity to ask me questions about the company and let me know what was on their minds.

Our meetings were all very informal. We took people out of their work settings for the meetings, served food, and made sure people understood that they were free to get up and walk around. By the end of the second hour, employees really began to share, not only about their relationships with the company but about their personal lives as well.

At one meeting, a person talked about having had a drug dependency. (This may have developed before we instituted our screening program or while he was working there.) He talked about the way the company had supported him as he entered a program and got clean. He said that because the company had saved his life, he was acting as a support for others at VOCA, who had similar problems either personally or in their families. There wasn't a dry eye in the room when he finished talking. Everybody stood and applauded him, including me. He had told his story in front of the boss.

In a company as large as VOCA, it would have been almost impossible to achieve that kind of familiarity without one-on-one opportunities. Time restraints don't allow it. This kind of recognition helps bridge the gap between workers and management.

Employee recognition can be tricky. As consultant and author Aubrey Daniels has noted, some common practices, such as Employee of the Month, can actually lead to negative results. Recognition of one person, for instance, can preclude recognition of others. It is not frequent enough to lead to long-term results, and in many organizations, it is not earned; it occurs when it is the employee's turn. None of this is very reinforcing.[*]

---

[*]Aubrey C. Daniels, Oops! 13 *Management Practices That Waste Time and Money (and what to do instead)*. (Atlanta, GA: Performance Management Publications, 2009), pp. 25-29.

Daniels recommends teaching employees about positive reinforcement as a scientific concept. Research has shown, for example, that reinforcement is most effective when it is personal (something the individual values), contingent on being earned, immediate and frequent. *

Recognition from both peers and management helps to bring out the best in people. It also does a lot for the person's image within the management structure. That person is seen as a comer. And since that person has gradually moved into the limelight, it's no surprise when he or she wins a promotion.

IDENTIFYING MANAGERIAL TALENT

Meetings, such as the one in which the employee shared his addiction story, can be helpful in identifying managerial candidates. It lets other employees know that the distance between us is not so great and that they have reason to be loyal to the company. Our most loyal managers are the ones we've promoted from within–people who will go the extra mile, and work the extra time for the sake of the services we provide.

If workers are made to feel that they can take responsibility

---

*Ibid. p. 33; Aubrey C. Daniels, *Bringing Out the Best in People: How to Apply the Astonishing Power of Positive Reinforcement* (New York: McGraw-Hill Education, 2016), pp. 64-73.

for their own behavior, those who are interested in developing managerial skills feel free to do so. As they break through the mythology of managers as a separate species, they realize, "I have skills. I like to lead. Maybe with some help, I can become a manager, too." They learn what it takes to be recognized by the company, and they recognize those attributes in other employees.

Peer recognition can be a useful tool in selecting candidates for entry-level supervisory positions. Employees are more accepting of a person who assumes a managerial role if they have participated with the manager in picking that person from among their own ranks. Peer recognition, far from being a popularity contest, is one of the best predictors of success.

> **Employees are more accepting of a person who assumes a managerial role if they have participated with the manager in picking that person from among their own ranks.**

A move up the supervisory ladder is just as risky for the appointing authority as it is for the employee who's making the climb. The person interviewing managerial candidates must guide them through the kind of self-analysis our imaginary mechanic went through before taking his promotion to service manager. He or she needs to make sure those prospective managers understand the risks and responsibilities specific to the positions they seek.

For a candidate at the level of program director, a first-line supervisory position, discussions about the job must be very concrete. And supervision of the newly appointed program director must be just as solid, bordering on invasive. Novice supervisors may buck at the seemingly incessant scrutiny, but they are better off with too much early watchfulness than too little, too late. The idea is to steer that program director to as many quick successes as possible. New supervisors should be able to say, "I made the right choice." Or, if it wasn't the right choice, they should have that realization early on, when they can still leave the position with their dignity intact.

Inevitably, first-line supervisors will develop a case of the jitters. Is it because the decision to take the job was an error, or are they simply nervous about their change in job status? How do they figure it out? How do their supervisors figure it out? Chances are that new program directors are unwilling to admit their failures. They want to show themselves and everyone else that they truly are right for the job. Managers who have watched closely will be able to sense how well things are going.

But let's go back a couple of steps. When you recognize an employee as a potential supervisor, how was she tapped for the job? Did she show promise in a previous position? How were her skills developed? To allow the employee to experience what leading involves, give her the opportunity to practice leadership skills in a safe environment. Give her a special assignment, a specific area of supervision. Let her recognize her own skills, so the change from clinician to manager, if it comes, will be less abrupt. This will give both of you the chance to assess her ability to exercise the qualities necessary for more encompassing managerial responsibilities.

Taking charge of one event or project may be enough; that's as much responsibility as some employees will ever want. But that one bite of responsibility will give the employee a taste of what it's like to sit on the manager's side of the desk, letting her know that being a supervisor isn't as easy as it may appear. It will also help break down the we-they barrier between managers and line employees. That barrier is strengthened when the only way to take charge is to have a title or role change. By inviting a number of people to oversee a variety of projects, you comfortably smudge the line.

Middle management is the hardest job in any organization. Middle managers are like middle children–they operate between executives and first-line supervisors. They're neither fish nor fowl, neither the adults in the corporate family nor the youngsters. They're in limbo. In addition, middle managers often become scapegoats. At the same time they're taking direction from executives higher up the line, they're also responsible for interpreting those directions for subordinate level supervisors. When communication goes awry, they're the ones who take the heat. And when budget cuts occur, they're the first to feel the ax.

If middle managers are simply note-passers, if their job is to take directives from the top and pass those directives on to the subordinate-level management staff without explanation, they are truly useless. Their job should be to make clear the policies and procedures that give rise to change, and ensure that directives can be followed at mid-level. They should be the coalescing point for ideas and changes that come up from the ranks of workers and first-line supervisors. They should be the stimulus for organizational change.

What you want to look for in choosing middle managers is the maturity to take unsophisticated responses or initiatives from supervisors and staff people, and convert those ideas, feelings and concerns into digestible pieces that executives can eat, enjoy and use. Keep in mind that all top executives were once middle managers.

Human service workers often bounce from agency to agency to work their way up managerial levels. There seems to be a magical quality about coming in from another agency or another state. So managers must carry along a portfolio, similar to a writer's or artist's, to demonstrate that they can be successful in positions beyond entry level, that they are prepared to assume higher-level management responsibilities.

It is the executives' job to create an environment in which

managers may experiment with top-level functions in the same way a manager helps program directors try out managerial functions. Top executives can then look within their own organizations for people with the qualifications they need.

But sometimes top-level executives are overly protective of their own positions. More often than not, they're older than other executives and managers. They fear the up-and-coming young folks who threaten their authority. They wonder if they still have what it takes, both personally and professionally. They find it more difficult to nurture their subordinates than they did when they were young.

In a society such as ours that places so much value on youth, older people seem to be thought of as throwaways. How can they help but feel threatened by the younger folks coming into their work arena? But as our society continues to age, we must learn to recognize the lessons older workers can teach us. And older managers, in turn, must learn to help those who follow in their footsteps.

MENTORING THE NEW MANAGER

My boss was in the hospital for cancer surgery during the first staff meeting of my first supervisory position. I was a New Yorker transplanted in South Carolina and new to the agency. I wasn't even sure where my office was. I was on my own.

My boss had told me that the department was out of control, and I was hired to whip things back into shape. And, indeed, I had noticed how loose everything was: People came to work when they wanted to, left when they wanted to, dressed the way they wanted to and chatted in their offices. I was scared, and I wasn't about to let anybody take advantage of my inexperience. My first comment at the meeting was, "I'm really glad to be here. You can expect me to run a tight ship." I paid for that mistake for years.

The ink was barely dry on my graduate degree when I took that job. I was 25 and full of myself. I didn't understand the culture of the agency or the culture of the South, so it was easy to make mistakes. Had there been a mentor at my side, I would have learned why the agency was the way it was. I would have known about Hilda, who had been there for 12 years and wanted my job. I would have known about Mary, who had a drinking problem. I would have had the information I needed to help me be more sensitive.

In the old trades, mentoring was a recognized part of a job. Masters passed along their crafts to journeymen, who oversaw apprentices. Unfortunately, we no longer have job descriptions for mentors, but we should–especially in human services. We are called to human services because we like to take care of other people. So let's take care of each other.

Moving into a managerial position is like moving to another part of the world. Imagine yourself suddenly thrust into the middle of another country. You need to eat, get a drink of water, and go to the bathroom, but a different language can complicate simple requests. You might, for instance, ask, "Where should I get off the bus?" In a certain context, you could accent the words incorrectly and insult the person you are talking to. What a relief it is if somebody comes up to you and says, "I'm going to help you through your first couple of weeks here. I'm going to help whenever I think you need help, even if you don't think you do."

Immediate feedback is essential as a person develops new skills. Sure, it's possible to survive without that support, but no one should have to tough it out alone. I did the job I was hired to do, and I was very successful, but I stepped over a lot of staff bodies to do it. Many years later, I still wonder if perhaps I destroyed capable people whom a mentor could have guided me to nurture instead. No one can smooth out all the bumps in the road. But a good mentor should be able to pull out the spikes that can pierce the new manager's heart.

Sitting in a coffee shop the other day, I overheard two young people complain about their bosses at a marketing firm in Chicago. They went on and on, complaining about how their jobs lacked any direction and quality oversight. What came to my mind immediately was that although many human service employees are poorly managed, this problem also occurs in every other sector of business. The point here is that we share the same issues that other businesses deal with on a regular basis. Good management practices apply in all areas of services and businesses alike. Untrained, ineffective managers will produce inadequate services and business results, which will ultimately affect the quality they provide to their clients and customers.

TRAINING FOR MANAGERS

My first few supervisors had no management training. They were clinicians or had worked in other human service organizations. Although most of them meant well, they lacked the skills they needed to be effective managers. The result was a haphazard set of goals with no understanding of how to achieve them. The answer was training–and mentoring. Unfortunately, it seems that in today's environment, money for training is the first thing that is cut from tight budgets though it is often what new managers need.

Early in my career, the University of Alabama had a federal grant to teach management to senior administrators, who were, at that time, mostly employed in state institutions. Community programs for IDD (Intellectual and

Developmental Disabilities) clients were not widespread. My role at the facility that employed me was to develop community-based group homes for the few individuals the state determined were ready for less restrictive living environments. Again, I was flying "by the seat of my pants" since there were very few models illustrating how to make this happen.

The university offered a one-year management certificate program, made available to select managers in several states. I was extremely fortunate to be chosen for this experience. Prior to enrolling at the university, I had no management education whatsoever. My graduate degree in social work trained me to become an excellent psychotherapist, but the curriculum paid no attention to any aspect of management. Back then, anything associated with business was considered almost "evil."

The courses offered at the university were taught by professors from the School of Business, and I felt like I had landed on another planet. Our professors taught us about supervision, finance, budgeting, unions, HR issues, and employee selection and development. At that point, I'd been out of graduate school for about three years. I felt competent when applying the clinical approaches I had been taught, but business principles? Forget it! Some of my colleagues rebelled at the curriculum, but this was an awakening that would stay with me through the rest of my career. After being embarrassed about how little I knew, I quickly realized that learning sound management skills was a prerequisite for accomplishing anything of substance in my chosen field, or in any field, for that matter. There was a choice to be made. I could ignore what I was being taught and continue to rely on my clinical skills to see me through, or celebrate my ignorance, embrace this new wisdom, and commit to making it an essential part of my future skill set. I quickly discovered that management was a profession and, like any other, required a new base of information.

I also discovered that I needed to practice my new skills under the tutelage of a master if I could ever find one. After a long while, I discovered, to my chagrin, that no such person existed anywhere close to where I was working. What I did discover was the American Management Association (AMA), which changed everything for me. They offered practical management courses and produced a journal that I found invaluable.

So I took some vacation time and attended a number of courses for the beginning manager. Although I was the only human service manager enrolled, I discovered that my lack of training and preparation was shared by managers from many business fields, even folks with MBAs. I was not alone "floating in my sea of ignorance." There were many others who found themselves adrift and unsupported.

Aside from learning this new and exciting science of management, I gained a great deal of insight from my fellow students as we discussed real-life cases of companies that had great difficulties, due mostly to poor management practices. Unfortunately, treating symptoms of organizational dysfunction did nothing to identify the root causes of the problems. So I also developed a skill that allowed me to assess first and eventually solve organizational problems by understanding the dysfunctional systems and people that perpetuated them.

Those interested in honing their leadership skills can find several such management courses available from the AMA, colleges and universities as well as many online resources.

SELECTING EMPLOYEES FOR PROMOTION

It takes time to select someone whose addition to the workforce will benefit the organization and help it grow and develop in a new way. But as managers, we spend more time firing people than we do hiring them. For instance, when we fire someone, we have to document a problem, deliver a verbal warning, a written warning and a second written warning. However, we need to spend as much or more time and attention on the people we hire and keep. What we do instead is akin to giving a goodbye party for someone who's leaving and nothing for someone who's coming on board. We need to remember that the people we hire become members of our corporate families. Again, we've been rewarding the wrong behavior.

Before a candidate is chosen for promotion, management needs to consider with care the criteria that will be used to assess his or her fit into the new job. That involves a certain amount of soul searching within the company, so the criteria will vary based on the answers to the following questions:

- What is the promotion all about?
- Is the person to replace someone who has left?
- Is the agency developing a new area for which this person will be responsible?
- Is a job being created especially to take advantage of an individual's unique skills?
- Is the promotion simply a token of acknowledgment of many years of service?
- How does a particular candidate fit the bill?
- What does the candidate expect from the promotion? (It's important to find out what the job means to that person, to make sure his or her understanding of it meshes with the company's.)

Finally, it is important to determine how that person's performance will be assessed at the end of a year. The best way to develop an evaluative instrument is with the participation of the person who will fill the job. It's easier for managers to develop a job description after assessing the bottom-line outcome indicators–to work backward– than it is to develop the job description and assess a year later whether or not the particulars have been met. By discussing outcome indicators, managers can build a job description that allows the person in the job to achieve the proper outcome.

The function of every job needs to be personalized. That way the person who takes the job is automatically the best fit since he or she has the skills and the personal-ity required to do it well. Personality is, in fact, an important part of the equation: What is the candidate's "collegiality quotient" with regard to people in similar jobs in the agency with whom he or she must interact? By that standard, the candidate for the position must be one who can fit into the organization as it exists, assuming that it is a healthy one. It doesn't mean, however, promoting employ-ees using a cookie cutter model. Rather managers need to trust their gut feelings about the qualified people wishing to join the corporate family. What makes those gut feel-ings trustworthy? The manager's ability to see through outer trappings, such as gender and ethnicity, and view each person as a unique candidate with a special reason for wanting the job.

> **The function of every job needs to be personalized so that the person who takes the job is automatically the best fit.**

Like any family, a company or agency will have its "odd-balls." But the decision to hire an unconventional employee must also be a conscious one. I, for example, was one of those "misfits." The South Carolina agency I worked for hired me to light fires.

I was not a Southerner and had no old-boy network to answer to. In fact, I had no understanding of the culture. But that was part of my appeal. Management wanted someone who would stick out. Hilda, with her 12 years' experience, didn't get the job because she would have maintained the status quo. The agency consciously decided to hire a maverick, and, my opening blunder aside, the strategy worked. In three years, I transformed a residential facility from what looked like a concentration camp into a place where people with disabilities could live comfortably and have access to their first community programs.

So I'm not suggesting harmony at all costs. I'm recommending that you know the cultural effect a new person or a newly promoted person is going to have on your organization and that you plan for it purposefully. Your agency can never again be the same once you make a change. Be in control of that. Develop criteria that serve the agency needs, not in the distant future, but in the present.

THE ART OF DELEGATION

Earlier in this book, I noted that managing is about influencing. Delegation is a large part of this function. Ideally, the managerial relationship works because the manager celebrates the fine work of the person to whom he or she delegated responsibility. "Because you do such excellent work, and because I allowed you to work as you do, we're better off than if I had done the job myself. You did it better than I could." Notice that the assessment is not, "You did it as well"; it is, "You did it better." That's 100,000 miles from, "I'm the best person for this job, but now my job is to find somebody who won't screw it up." Or, "I need to find someone who will screw it up so that I can step in and save it."

The person to whom the job is delegated must participate in deciding the criteria necessary for accomplishing identified results. Allow that person to say, in effect, "I'm giving you my thoughts on how I can fulfill this assignment beyond anybody's wildest expectations. As I perform this job, I see other things I can do to make the outcome greater than it might have been. I'm going to take those things and add them into the mix."

Say you need a loaf of bread, and the person to whom you delegate the responsibility for buying it comes back with banana bread. Most likely you were expecting whole wheat, but look what you get instead. It's bread, but it's different. It looks different, smells different and tastes different. It certainly was not what you expected, and it might require making adjustments, but if you like it, you're delighted.

In the best scenarios, that's what happens. Another mind, a dedicated, intelligent mind, removes the blinders of the delegating authority and applies a new set of experiences to the problem. If the problem is delegated to a committee, the experiential possibilities and the possible solutions multiply by the number of people assigned to resolve the issue. The art of managing is in seeing that potential. As managers train supervisors, they need to help them see that potential in others.

Another quality of a good manager is the ability to take pride in the work of others. As a manager, your responsibility goes beyond the perimeters of your own body. You need to recognize the value of other people. You have an obligation to be greater than you would be without their help. It's a risk.

See yourself as the conductor of an orchestra. Given your direction and understanding of each musician's individual input, the orchestra learns to play a symphony in a way you've never heard before. It's almost beyond your anticipation of what was possible.

That's the ideal. It's achievable at times and what we need to strive for. In fact, it's the most enjoyable, fulfilling experience you'll ever have.

SUCCESSION PLANNING

No one likes to think about becoming disabled or dying; we all want to think of ourselves as immortal. Even in the days of living wills and prepaid funerals, many don't want to think about their final arrangements though it's quite sensible. Likewise, in not-for-profit companies and agencies, succession planning is often given too little thought. If an agency has few debts, there's no one looking over its shoulder to see that it's managed in a way that enables it to continue. That job falls to the board of directors, whose function is not to run day-to-day operations but to set and oversee policy. The board must demand succession planning from the people who make the agency run.

In private industry, banks and other investors will push for succession planning. They want to know that the company will be there in 25 years, long after the executive has left or retired. In a publicly traded company, this is an even greater concern. Now, in addition to bankers, the executive has stockholders watching what he or she is doing. In fact, even in the most successful publicly traded organizations, stocks plummet after a change at the top if that change was not planned for. "What was going on before the change?" stockholders want to know. If the late executive was physically ill, was he or she mentally competent to run the company?

Whether they are proprietary or not-for-profit, organizations too often fail after the death of the top executive. They fail because the executive's ego insisted that "Nobody else can do what I do." Executives must plan for their own replacement. That means nurturing the people under them and letting them pick up the management skills they need to move up. Of course, that means creating environments necessary for growth.

The named successor must work in partnership with the top executive to make sure he or she acquires the skills to make the transition as smooth as possible. But both must be willing to admit, if necessary, that the partnership should be dissolved. They may very well find that the successor-elect, though outstanding in every other way, does not adapt well to the skills required to lead the company.

The person likely to succeed an executive usually has a lot to learn before taking over or buying the business. That person has to take his or her current skills and add ones for the executive challenge. He or she also must know the executive well enough and have the ability to walk in one day and say, "I don't want this." It doesn't make sense to saddle someone with an eternal commitment when it's impossible to see that far down the road. The person picked as successor today may not want the job ten years from now. But the top executive won't know that unless he or she talks to the successor-elect frequently and keeps tabs on that person's interest and ability to take over.

The decision about a replacement involves constant re-evaluation. Insurance agents insist on frequent updates to their clients' coverage to make sure it meets the clients' ever-changing needs. Top executives should look on succession planning in a similar way. The company's needs are different today than they were five years ago, and in another five years they will be different than they are now. The executive must also be able to accept the fact that the organization will change under new leadership, that after a while he or she might only vaguely recognize it as the company it was before.

Ultimately, I sold VOCA to another organization. I hoped and prayed that it would be better than I left it. I chose a buyer that would have the same values I would have chosen in a successor, but I must still understand that the new executive or organization will imprint the company with different values.

Being chosen to fill a founder's shoes can be a curse. Whether or not their portrait hangs above the successor's desk, the founder's presence is felt all the same. I heard a story about a guy who left the company he'd started to his son after signing on to a heavy debt. The son ran the business into the ground. How could the father deal with that? What would I do today if a disgruntled banker or shareholder were to call and tell me the new company was sending the remains of VOCA down the tubes? Nothing. I have to let it go down the tubes if that's what happens.

In any case, as long as you are leading your organization, you have to keep planning and mentoring for the time you will no longer be there. If you know that you have a terminal disease that leaves you only a year to live, you would have no time to prepare your successor. You would be forced to pass along to him or her a half-baked cake. Certainly, some tragedy could befall you, but your intention must be to give yourself time to bake that cake so that your successor, who helped mix in the ingredients, can take it and serve it up as he or she desires. That's how companies grow best, not by fits and starts, but through transitions so smooth that while people may sense differences they don't know quite what they are.

Managing Relationships with External Organizations

TRADE ORGANIZATIONS

Trade organizations are associations of businesses, institutions or professionals in particular trades, academics or specialties. They are usually founded and funded by members and engage in a variety of activities, including support for members, education, specialized news and information, conferences, mentor programs and even lobbying.

Good trade organizations can provide human service managers with a broad overview of the most pressing issues that affect the field on a state or national level. They help agencies articulate problems and present solutions similar agencies have developed for similar problems. They also help executives keep abreast of state and national regulatory trends as well as of changes in law that affect the industry.

Because we are so client oriented, many people in human

services have had little experience flexing collective muscle to shape the outcomes of regulations. We tend to be caught up in the work of our small agencies and feel isolated from one another, thus having no collective identity. And because we often have little discretionary money, we don't have much in our budgets for memberships–and we get what we pay for. We need to dig deeper in our pockets and participate more actively if we want trade associations that advocate for us consistently.

Becoming active in a trade association that brings together service providers dealing with the same issues offers you an opportunity to become an effective agent for change as long as there is a willingness to work together as a group to get things done. As a unified trade group along with powerful advocacy organizations and the support of involved families, you can get the attention of rule makers and legislators that have the ultimate power to reorient their funding priorities. Allying yourself with organizations also adds a great deal of credibility to your efforts. Once funders understand how your financial stability improves services that they are already funding, the barriers to change can be reduced

Organizations that work for clients, such as TASH, an international leader in disability advocacy, advocate for individual rights but do very little for the agencies that serve those individuals. On the other hand, the American Association on Intellectual and Developmental Disabilities

(AAIDD) and the National Association of Qualified Intellectual Disability Professionals (NAQ) provide educational presentations and events, publications and networking opportunities, such as conferences.

Most organizations that deal with human services were founded around academics, which makes sense since most people within the profession have strong academic backgrounds and advanced degrees. Yet service providers have pragmatic needs as well. In recent years, these associations have included more and more programming on operating and maintaining organizations from the point of view of day-to-day operations and from a business orientation. We must be willing to support those organizations that serve all of our needs both financially and through our active participation.

Many of us are hesitant to act too much like a "business." By creating true, hard-boiled, lobbying trade associations, they fear, we would remove ourselves from the cloak of virtue. This has nothing to do with virtue, but rather with good management and how to deliver our services more effectively.

If a business continues to make a profit over a long time period, the assumption is that it's providing a quality product that people are going to buy and pay for. Yet such success can be ephemeral in a time of rapid tech and service innovation. We have seen Amazon put retailers, even good ones, out of business, and Apple upend stalwart brands, such as

Nokia and Motorola. We have seen grocery specialty stores, such as Trader Joe's and Whole Foods, force older grocery chains to improve their prepared food and produce sections.

These changes are the result of classic competition. Yet the market for human services, as the market for health care, often operates differently. For one thing, there is the phenomenon of managed care that involves contractual arrangements with paying entities, such as government and insurance companies. Fees are set through capitation agreements that provide a set amount for each client and the cost of treatment is monitored by a managing entity. These arrangements can severely affect an agency's ability to innovate and provide needed services.

Meanwhile, politicians continue to call for decreasing resources for health care and allied services even though we know needs are increasing. We have no choice but to become competitive and sensitive to the marketplace. This is happening, to some extent, in the hospital marketplace. For instance, we now see ads for hospital systems and health-care centers we would not have seen in the recent past. At the same time, new models of service, such as urgent care centers and drugstore clinics, especially in more populated areas, provide care in more cost effective manners.

It would be great if funders made decisions based on agencies' effectiveness, and if rate structures rewarded efficient service delivery. But that isn't the way it works. Certainly, there are means tests for our services. Agencies that harm people or that don't offer appropriate services are rarely encouraged through continued funding. But what happens if there are no agencies to pick up the slack? In a rural area, for example, if there's only one funded agency, it has to be intolerably grim before it's defrocked since there's nothing else to take its place.

We must be more competitive. Look at the accounting profession. Accountants compete constantly for available clients, through pricing as well as through the broad-based resources they make available to people. I'd like to see that happen in human services. Sound scary? It probably does to those of us who fear that competitiveness would change our mission from considering the best interests of the client to making a profit. But those motives are not mutually exclusive. If agencies are allowed to show that the best interests of the client are in everyone's best interest, that people should be adequately rewarded for their commitment to quality, then the marketplace will change and clients will have a greater variety of agencies to choose from.

Fortunately, we have a number of ways to check on the worthiness of businesses. In addition, to the Better Business Bureau and Consumer Reports, the internet enables consumers who may know nothing about a particular product to assess the best buy for the price. We have Yelp and a host of online services that allow people to post both ratings and stories about their experiences. We owe the public some indicator to use when assessing our services.

Some trade associations set standards for their members, a practice that human services professionals should emulate by empowering self-policing trade groups. If we don't keep watch over ourselves, others will do it for us, people who may not understand what we do and who will continue to strap us with massive regulatory restraints.

CONSULTANTS

Benefits packages can add a large percentage to the cost of keeping full-time people on the payroll. As agencies find it more difficult to pay for those benefits, they will begin to use more consultants. The hourly rate for a consultant is higher than that of a full-time person, but since the consultant has no permanent position, he or she is not entitled to vacation time, sick leave, medical insurance, or any other benefit an agency might offer its employees.

You should be constantly reassessing the workings of your agency. As you do, ask yourself, "Why are all my staff people in their jobs? Am I getting the best I can for the money I'm spending?" Corporate downsizing in other industries is a result of managers asking those questions. Companies that don't look critically at their use of manpower are going out of business; they can no longer afford to spend money aimlessly. Unfortunately, we in human services deal with the same economic realities. Therefore, we will suffer the ax as well if we don't ask ourselves those tough questions, get as much as we can out of the people we hire, and continually readjust our organizational designs to produce the most quality for the lowest cost.

A position that was essential to your agency six years ago may not be necessary now. Or, even if the work is still there, it may not require a full-time person. You may be able to hire that work out on a per-project, per-consultant basis.

Consultants work in a competitive environment that full-time workers needn't worry about. To win your contract, Consultant A must defend his or her work against Consultants B through Z. To win your business again, Consultant A must perform to standards rarely applied to full-time workers.

Therefore, your choice of a consultant is very important. You need to check out that person as thoroughly as you would someone you planned to hire full time. If you hire a consultant, you have an equal share in the quality of his or her work. If the consultant makes a mistake, you are the one held responsible.

A consultant's primary objective should be to work himself out of a job. Your contract with that person should spell out a specific purpose and a reasonable time limitation. It should also include a "not-to-exceed" clause. Consultancy costs can escalate quickly. The way to control them is to specify a maximum number of hours per week or per month for which you'll pay the consultant. If the contract says no more than 10 hours per week, for example, and the consultant puts in 15, you're responsible to pay only for the agreed-upon 10 hours unless you specifically give approval for extra time.

Make it clear to consultants that their relationships with you are production-oriented. Let them know up-front that you will continue to call on them if they produce the results or services you agreed on, and that if they don't they'll never hear from you again.

In a small agency, you may not have the budget for top-level consultants, but by pooling resources with other agencies, you might be able to afford the best neurologist in your area or the best psychopharmacologist in the country. As a consortium, you might take advantage of folks you could never consider on your own. It's an idea that has worked many times.

UNIONS

The role of unions has evolved. In many cases, working conditions have improved in factories and other businesses as both government regulation and social sensibility demand a greater level of safety. Unions still seek to protect the rights of workers, yet as they have grown, they have sometimes become politicized by taking positions on issues, such as work rules, minimum wage, benefits, whether or not union membership should be mandatory in an organization, and more. At the same time, while adversarial relationships remain in many instances, in others, union leadership and management have reached cooperative agreements for the greater good and survival of the organization.

Most employees see very little distinction between the people who run a company and the company itself, so their attitudes toward executives and managers will probably play a role in how they feel about unionization. To the people who meet you, you are that organization. This can add another layer to your job, which already shuttles between fundraising and keeping the toilets working. You have to show that being an astute executive does not preclude your being a kind and loving person.

When we first talked to VOCA employees about budgets, we realized that anything that had to do with money frightened them. Even though they knew money had to come from somewhere, they would rather not have to think about it. But when we allowed them not to think about money, we also allowed them to demand more than there was to give. Because they didn't participate in creating parameters within which money could be spent, that is, acceptable budgets, they found it easier to ask for more, especially from me. I'm sure they thought that I had an unlimited pool of money as the owner of the company.

The rich boss image is a well-established character in American mythology. From Daddy Warbucks to Jeff Bezos, we think of the boss as powerful and somewhat distant. What a hard pill that is to swallow for a human service professional who becomes a manager, who now represents the "power elite." "When did I become elite?" the former clinician wonders. "When did I become powerful?"

VOCA went through a number of difficult labor relations issues, not the least of which was a two-month strike at one of our homes that thankfully ended in everybody's best interest. I believe the union would now agree that the issues involved were not strike worthy, but at the time, they mistakenly expected VOCA to capitulate, so they did. The battle itself became the focus of the strike, and winning was everything. The issues took a back seat.

Our corporate lawyer saw a way out of the impasse and

suggested the "combatants" sit down together to discuss the issues that divided us confidentially. I met with the president of the union, and we solved the dispute in three hours. I hate to think what could have happened had we not been able to reach an agreement. But the minute we sat down at the table, we could see in each other's face that we had had enough. There were neither winners nor losers in the way we ended the strike. In fact, one of the most important items we agreed on was to form a labor management alliance that would prevent this kind of craziness from happening again. We developed a trusting relationship. He knew that my managers and I were not out to harm his workers, and we both knew that our success depended on the other. After that, it became easier for us to sit beside one another and talk rather than feel the need to stand at odds.

The masks we wear, whether they are those of labor or those of management, are very hard to put down, yet success requires we do just that. Often it requires going back to a time before emotions escalated out of control. That was what the union president and I did in our meeting; we agreed to start fresh.

The issue of whether to seek representation comes up for employees in many types of industries today, including health care and human services. The union embraced by some of VOCA's employees specialized in healthcare workers in private industry. We found unions to be a double-edged sword, a blessing as well as a curse. On one hand, we discovered that union contracts made it easier for us to develop consistent management practices throughout the corporation. We were able to standardize wages and benefits. On the other hand, unions sometimes bring work rules that may or may not be the best way to operate.

At any rate, unions may very well be part of your organization, and if they are, you must develop effective labor-management partnerships. One way is to talk to companies that have been approached by unions, have unions or have decided to accept union contracts. What issues came up? Did they oppose unionization or welcome it. What happened?

You need to think through what your position might be if approached. You also need to find a good labor relations attorney, who understands the nature of the unions that might seek to organize your employees, what methods they are likely to employ and what your options are as management. It's easier than you can imagine to commit an unfair labor practice. You could unwittingly break a rule you didn't even know about.

Go to a seminar–go to several seminars–and hire a consultant to help you understand what unionization might mean for your company. I did not take a course in labor relations in graduate school, but such courses exist in human resources, business, and other curricula. If I had taken such a course, it would have been useful.

WORKING WITH GOVERNMENT OFFICIALS

Today, private industry is carrying out many services once handled by government agencies. In several instances, government has become the monitor rather than the provider. A partnership is essential for the system to work, but unfortunately, human service professionals and government officials often seem to speak different languages.

On one hand, many state regulators have no operational or business experience. They grew up in government, so they don't always understand the business needs of private service providers. Government must realize that, if we are to encourage the kind of competition in the industry that ensures the most effective use of service dollars, we must be allowed to make a reasonable profit. (Call it a return on investment if your agency is not-for-profit; it's all the same.) On the other hand, it can be difficult for us, as human service providers, to understand the government's responsibility to be the ultimate safety net while options remain limited and resources are scarce.

In addition to the lack of understanding, we, as human service providers, are not always clear about our needs when we select the people with whom we wish to communicate. We must be clear–and we must make our pleas to those we think will listen and help. One way to do this is by finding legislative candidates we feel comfortable endorsing and working for tirelessly. It is not enough that they be friendly to our industry; they must represent good government thinking. There is sometimes a tendency to view politicians as villains. Yet many of the men and women willing to take on political office deserve our honest attention and scrutiny. More importantly, they deserve our support.

We must understand that even the most well-meaning legislator may find it difficult to take the risks, associated with running for office and doing the job once elected. That doesn't mean these people don't care. They do. But it's our job, as we lobby for what we need, to understand their needs as we ask them to understand ours. If a senator is up for re-election and you approach him or her to sponsor a massive, controversial piece of legislation, you should expect to be disappointed. The senator doesn't want to get behind anything that might cost any votes. Whether liberal or conservative, he or she wants to be seen, as much as possible, as an ally, someone who ought to be sent back to Washington or the state capital.

When contacting your representative or senator, understand that state legislators are in one mindset when visiting their districts and another when they are at the statehouse. Their attention is on their constituents. If your needs depend on a relationship with this particular legislator, send someone from the district to make the approach. Or make your approach when the legislator is at the statehouse and likely to take on a more global outlook.

Don't be afraid to challenge a legislator's misperceptions about the kind of work you do. In fact, rather than moan and groan that the legislator does not understand or doesn't care, knock on the door and say, "I heard what you said about such-and-such. I have some facts you might want to listen to." More than likely the official will listen though you may not change his or her mind. At least you'll know another viewpoint

> **Don't be afraid to challenge that legislator's misperceptions about the kind of work you do.**

may be considered. However, do make sure you make the approach armed with hard evidence. Shaking your finger and saying, "How dare you be so insensitive to ...," will get you nowhere, and chaining yourself to the doorknob will only lead to anger. You can be far more effective in the legislator's office or over lunch, talking person to person.

It's also important to know legislators' staff people. They are the ones who do the legwork, who have the time to visit your program and see what you're doing. They are the ones who synthesize the data and help legislators decide what positions to take on various issues. Often they are young party loyalists–possibly personal family or friends of a legislator– and frequently lack experience. They need to be educated.

Political action committees, or PACs, are another way of moving legislators to consider specific issues. PACs take various small pots of money and turn them into one big pot of money for contributions to candidates who support the issues that concern them. They use measurable criteria to screen candidates. The questions they ask a candidate need to be specific enough that, if the person is elected, the PAC can later say, "You told us you were going to do this, this and this. Have you? If not, why?"

No matter which way you choose to make your point known to legislators, you must find out what supports they need to accomplish the work that interests you. And if a legislator you're working with tries and fails–after all, on the federal level, each senator is one of 100, each representative one of 435–you need to be able to say, "You really did keep your promise to us. Even though the legislation didn't pass, you gave it a great effort." You need to thank the legislator and offer your assistance next time around when the political environment might be more congenial.

Sometimes it may not be just a legislative battle that's lost. At some point, you're bound to throw your support behind a candidate who loses a bid for election. How you treat that person after his or her loss is very important because someone whose lifeline is politics will be back. And that person will remember who stayed behind when everyone else skipped off to the victory party.

THE PUBLICLY FUNDED SYSTEM

Any publicly funded program is a reflection of the political realities of its time. A program such as Medicaid, for example, which is a source of funding for people with disabilities, has seen many changes since it was enacted in 1965. As people with disabilities live longer, and the instance of disabilities grows, such programs become more expensive.

People with permanent disabilities are likely to be served by some kind of program throughout their lives. As human service professionals, we have to be aware of the escalating costs in providing services. In order to be prudent fiduciaries of public funds, we also need to help the public understand ways of preventing many of the disabilities from occurring in the first place.

It is within our power in this country to reduce the risks of disabilities substantially. Certainly we're not going to prevent all disabilities, but we know, to a large extent, what causes them. The general public, however, does not understand that education and good health care, though expensive, cost far less than caring for people for 50, 60 or 80 years because of congenital disabilities that were preventable. Therefore, we human service professionals are morally bound not only to advocate for the best services available to people once they have a disability, but also to say to the public, "We have ways to keep this from happening if only we provide adequate funding for prevention."

There's an unspoken belief in this country that people in need of public assistance somehow deserve to be in that condition. The fact is that most people who receive assistance are in the workforce. They are minimally employed in service industries, retail or undependable seasonal jobs. As the digital revolution progresses, many jobs requiring less skilled workers no longer exist, or people may lack the resources to find better work options. Some people may be ripping off the system, but they are the exception.

The underlying message is that the public does not consider itself to be its brother's keeper as it once did. We've lost our sense of community, a trend heightened as many people lose themselves in digital devices and home-based entertainment. We isolate ourselves. We've lost our interdependence. Depression is a growing problem in this country, perhaps in part because people have no support systems.

This is why direct support employees in our agencies are so important. They are often the people who provide the part of the support system that is personally experienced by those who need our services. They are also workers who cannot be replaced digitally and whom we owe a living wage.

However, human service managers need to understand the political realities when advocating for programs or funding. It means working feverishly to elect politicians sympathetic to programs for the people we serve, and also voicing logical arguments for adequate funding that answer questions that may never even be asked. Politicians with less and less money to allocate hear more and more demands. Why should one program get funded and not another? Clearly, that is the issue. There simply isn't enough money to go around. If one program receives funding, another must be cut. Managers, who are not vociferous, knowledgeable advocates, will fall victim to poorly developed public policies—and so will their clients.

The managers at VOCA Corp. saw themselves as actively involved in advocating and informing the public and their legislators, not just to grow our business but enable us to provide the services our clients needed. We created our name, in fact, from the middle of the word adVOCAcy. This helped us to promote both ourselves and what we do.

But what are we advocating for? What quality of life should people with disabilities expect to have? Most in the general public would agree that they should be fed, clothed and housed away from the elements. Then what? The Americans with Disabilities Act articulates in no uncertain terms that society may not act prejudicially against people with disabilities. However, it is harder to legislate morality. How much are we willing to pay for the dignity of a person with a physical or mental disability? How much if the person's "disability" is cultural, economic or environmental? Where will the money come from? A well-orchestrated social system can support people for a short time while they develop the independence to become contributors to society.

A colleague in Pennsylvania told me the story of an Amish child born with multiple disabilities. The doctors, psychologists, psychiatrists and social workers gave the girl's family their prognosis of her abilities: she had a severe intellectual disability and would never work. The girl's mother asked, "Can she use her hands?"

"Yes," the professionals answered, "she can use her hands." The mother smiled.

"Why are you smiling?" one physician asked. "This is a very sad time."

"Because she can knit and crochet," the mother responded.

Before that child even left the hospital, she had a role to fill within her society. Her family wasn't concerned with what she couldn't do, but with what she could do. Had the answer been, "No, she can't use her hands," her family and community still would have found some way to enable her to contribute. And it wasn't just their altruistic way of making another person feel good. To continue as a community, the Amish must include everyone.

American society as a whole lacks that ethic. Many ethnic groups come to this country with a sense of community that dwindles as successive generations pull away from the immigrant parent, grandparent or great-grandparent. Urbanized America displaces people from their communities and throws them together in ways that mean nothing to them, moving them into subdivisions where they don't know their neighbors' names. It's not surprising that people don't concern themselves with their neighbors when they don't know who they are or care to find out.

We need to make massive changes within our society to remedy the way we treat each other. Maybe, like the Amish baby, people with disabilities hold the answer. They teach us that we can be compassionate, that we can make a difference in people's quality of life. If we can do it for people with disabilities, why can't we do it for everyone?

LOBBYING

If your organization receives any financial support from any level of government, you need to give serious thought to the following facts. People who run for office, by necessity, spend a great deal of time fundraising. In fact, members of Congress spend countless hours a week in their political offices calling constituents and others to ask for money. Representatives, who run every two years, never stop making these calls. Before we criticize this behavior, we need to understand the facts. Because of the high cost of media advertising and other campaign expenses, it takes a lot of money to run a viable campaign. Depending on their locations and political situations, House candidates may need millions of dollars to run their campaigns, Senate candidates need many times that. State office seekers are in the same situation with gubernatorial candidates in highly visible races rivaling congressional campaigns. In addition, even if funds are not being spent, current office holders want enough cash on hand to scare off any would-be competitors.

Is it any surprise then that even independently wealthy candidates for public office are constantly raising money? You and I might agree that this system has many flaws–not the least of which is that a candidate whose ideals appeal to us has no chance of winning without adequate financial support. Nevertheless, it is today's political reality.

As a private company, we were a catalyst in helping our colleagues realize the benefits of contributing to political campaigns. Campaign funding was ear-marked for those individuals who made the laws and passed the regulations that greatly affected our service delivery systems. Political contributions get you in the door so that you can present your issues. The only thing you get for your money is access, but without access you will be left out of the legislative process. You may hate the idea of "Pay to Play," but this is the way the political world works. If you choose not to "Play," don't complain about the resulting effect of poorly conceived laws and regulations that affect your professional life and the supports you are providing to those you serve.

Of course, if your agency has nonprofit tax status, which allows it to accept tax-exempt contributions, the agency itself will not be able to make direct political contributions. You, as an individual, however, are free to contribute or support candidates within legal campaign contribution limits.

In addition, your state association can play a vital role here by asking for contributions from members of the association and forming a political action committee or PAC. Obviously, you need to be involved in who gets these contributions and why. You need to get the "biggest bang for your buck!"

Choosing the correct legislator or governor to support will take some work. First, try to gain access to the most powerful person you can. That may be the Speaker of the House or the President of the Senate, and don't forget the governor. Look at their voting records and see if they have ever authored or supported legislation that you determine is supportive of what you want to accomplish.

Now, if the legislators or executives in power do not appear to have supported any social or human service programs, all is not lost. Find their positions on issues that got them elected. They may never have articulated their support for social programs, but have run their campaigns on fiscal accountability in government or on some other set of issues. Fiscal accountability is obviously a very popular theme.

Your entry point here is to demonstrate how efficient, well-managed programs can actually save money. If you can demonstrate that you are good stewards of the funds you receive and can demonstrate how accountable you are, you will most likely gain a receptive ear. Ask your government official to visit your program and see if he or she will set a date to do this.

And be careful what you wish for. Depending on the stature of the person you have invited, he or she may well bring the press along. Politicians live and die by the quality of their press coverage. Now, if you are careful and have planned this visit well, this could be a "home run." Know that you are opening yourself up to a very high level of visibility. If the press does come and you have had to deal with a negative issue, such as an angry neighbor, be ready to deal with the issue on the spot. If the story was reported in the press previously, the likelihood of your needing to explain and defend increases. Is this exposure worth the risk? Done correctly, you bet it is!

Why should you care about any of this? The fact is that you will not be able to deliver viable, quality services with insufficient funds. You can yell and scream all day about how terribly underfunded your agency is, but that behavior will get you nowhere.

WORKING WITH BUREAUCRACY

My company relied totally on Medicaid funds. As you know, these are federal funds that are matched by states and administered by various state agencies. We soon realized that it was the state's administration of those funds that really mattered. Aside from setting rates of reimbursement, states promulgate many regulations on how their money is to be spent. They decide who gets these funds and how recipients of these funds will be held accountable for their use. The "devil" is indeed in the detail of the regulations that states impose on providers. Sometimes these regulations are well thought out and fair, but, sad to say, they are often capricious and arbitrary, driven only by a need to

contain ever-escalating costs. Unfortunately, state administrators rarely have any real-life operating experience, so
the regulations that they write rarely reflect the realities of
actual program and service delivery. The result is that many
payment systems are woefully inadequate and rarely take
into account actual operating cost realities.

So what do you do? First, I suggest that you develop the
best relationships possible with everyone who funds and
regulates you. I mean, get to know these people as people.
Get them to tell you about their families, where they went
on vacation and what their hobbies are. This relationship
building will take time to mature since the premise of the
relationship is initially built on an adversarial model. I've
never met a surveyor who thought his or her job was to
compliment me on the excellent services I was providing.
Believe me, I know first-hand the benefits to be derived from
good relationships with people who held the fate of my program in their hands.

Your relationship with surveyors can start simply by offering
a cup of coffee and letting them know where the restroom is.
Of course, if you are delivering substandard services, having
a good relationship with your regulators will not and should
not help you. If, however, you are doing the best you can, are
proud of your service outcomes and can demonstrate your
results through accurate measures, you will most certainly
develop good relationships with regulators that will go a

long way toward helping them understand and appreciate the efforts you are making to deliver quality services.

We all know that we are serving individuals with varying physical, emotional, intellectual and mental disabilities. Unforeseen accidents and tragedies will happen, and having good relationships with the individuals who oversee and regulate your services will go a long way toward helping you and them deal with these unfortunate but predictable circumstances. I'm amazed at how few providers have collegial relationships with their surveyors. Treating them like the enemy and being defensive about their inspections will only serve to raise suspicions about you, your services and your operations. Conversely, appreciating them and the roles they must perform will go a long way toward improving quality communications between you and them.

> **Appreciating surveyors and the roles they must perform will go a long way toward improving quality communications between you and them.**

Once you have established a good rapport with your regulators, you can educate them about the difficult issues you are facing and solicit their advice on how to mitigate them. By the way, very few people ask their surveyors for their opinions on how to improve quality. Once they see that you value their opinions and that you see them as part of your team, relationships are bound to improve.

Some time ago, Ohio had a newly appointed Director of MR/DD,* who was convinced that all for-profit companies were bad and that they made their profits by short-changing the quality of the services they were delivering to their clients. After meeting with him several times, it was clear that he was not going to change his negative perception of me, our for-profit company or how we were spending the state money we were receiving for our programs. Out of complete desperation, I came up with a radical plan that changed my relationship with this gentleman.

I set up another meeting and told the director that it was obvious that his opinion, although incorrect, would never change. I told him that I was willing to give him all of our audited financial and tax statements and ask that he conduct a forensic audit of our company. After assuring him that I was not kidding, he agreed to do the audit. When I told my CFO what I had done, he almost had a heart attack. I asked him if we had anything to hide and if he was indeed convinced that every state dollar we had received was appropriately spent and accounted for. He, of course, agreed, and I hand-delivered all our records to the director's office myself. Be assured that before I made this "outrageous" offer, I was fully confident in our numbers and our accountability for all our expenditures. The audit took two months. I received a call from the director who wanted to meet as soon as possible. When I entered his office, he immediately shook my

---

*Mental Retardation/Developmental Disabilities

hand, thanked me for what I had done, saying that he had felt that I would never follow through on my commitment to him. The director said that the audit had found that everything I had told him previously had been true, and, to my amazement, he apologized for not believing me.

Then something wonderful happened. I asked the director if he had ever done an audit of his own department. He said he had not. I asked him if he would agree to compare and contrast the expenditures that the state was paying to run their own programs to my financials. I made sure that he knew that my financial information included everything from my salary, the salaries for all my staff, our cost of capital for housing, payments on our bank loans, our profit, etc. There was literally nothing that had been omitted from my financial statements. Knowing that the department audit would never occur, the director agreed to compile a list of what the state spent on the programs they were administering.

A month later, I got another call to attend another meeting. This meeting was by far the most cordial meeting I had ever had with this man. He said that his financial review disclosed that we were providing our service for less than half of what the state was spending. He recognized that our profit was derived from the administrative savings we were able to realize though efficient administration and management practices. We developed a level of mutual respect that lasted until his term was up and a new administration was appointed.

Our commitment to developing and maintaining good relationships with the people and entities that governed in every state in which we operated, proved to be not only beneficial to our company and its staff but also ultimately to the clients entrusted to our care.

Financial Considerations

7

FINANCIAL REALITIES

If you spend more money than you make, you will go out of business, plain and simple. Some years ago, a religious order of nuns in Ohio operated a program for individuals with disabilities. They always operated on the edge because they were convinced that since they were a religious order, they would continue to be funded by state revenues and donations. I had a friend who had a child with a severe disability, who was being served by this organization. He was a prominent lawyer in Columbus and gave the sisters thousands of dollars each year. Unfortunately, his daughter died, and my friend stopped donating to the program. Year after year, the sisters, who had no management experience, over-spent their revenue sources. Eventually, the quality of their services deteriorated and the State of Ohio had to revoke their license to operate. We were called in to serve the remaining residents in the program. No one ever thought the program would close its doors, but business realities are inflexible.

Most human service managers have little, if any, training in dealing with finances. Our discomfort with financial matters is obvious in the way we handle our personal finances, our checkbooks and our investments. Many of us find it painful to make any kind of decision that has to do with spending money. If we're lucky, we find spouses or friends who will take on that responsibility for us. More often than not, we're the victims in monetary dealings.

We also have terrible sales resistance. We want everybody to like us, and salespeople pick up on that. We hate to negotiate. We hate to haggle. We like to get our money's worth, but we're uncomfortable with the effort it takes.

There are some interesting models of how to think about finances on the popular reality show "Shark Tank." On the show, people pitch their ideas to potential investors who always ask the same type of questions: "What are your costs of doing business? Where does your revenue come from and is it sustainable? What will you do with the money you are asking from us? How will I, as an investor, make money and what is my return?"

Those who cannot quickly answer these basic questions are quickly dismissed from "The Tank," sometimes without a lot of understanding or compassion. If a business is awarded an investment by one or more of the Sharks, the investor Shark will own a portion of the company and work to protect his or her investment. In addition to providing capital, the investor will serve as a mentor.

Do you have "investors"? Sure, you do! They are every entity that funds you whether they are public or private. Every financial report you submit details the money you receive and how you spend it. The admonition heard from the investors on Shark Tank is always, "Know your numbers." Sometimes companies that come on the show are so "in love" with their product that they pay very little attention to their numbers (i.e., how sustainable their market and revenue are, and what return they are getting from their sales).

If you really understand your numbers, you will be head and shoulders over your less informed competition. Accurate financial information is an essential body of information that drives the viability and sustainability of your operations. If you don't know your numbers and more importantly how to use them, you will fail. I don't care how great your service concept is. If you don't know your numbers, you will go out of business.

> **If you really understand your numbers, you will be head and shoulders over your less informed competition.**

When I started VOCA Corp., it was painful for me to realize how ignorant I was about fiscal issues. But lacking financial skills, I used a skill that I did have—the ability to network. I developed relationships with fiscal managers I could trust.

When I interviewed the person who would become VOCA's chief financial officer, the first thing I said to him was, "This will probably be unlike any interview you've ever had. I'm not going to ask questions about what you know. I'm going to tell you how little I know." Our focus in the interview was the kind of relationship I wanted to have with the person in that position. Would I be able to reveal my ignorance to him without feeling foolish? Would he guide me toward the information I needed, and advise me on reading materials and seminars? Would he be willing to explain things to me over and over and over again?

Obviously, our future CFO's qualifications went beyond his collegiality quotient. I checked out his technical credentials with the accounting firm he worked for at the time, which happened to do our audits. Accounting firms are wonderful, no-cost resources for talent. Most CPAs who join accounting firms never become partners, so the firms gladly place qualified people in positions with other companies. They have a vested interest in doing so. The firm with which we worked, for example, wanted us to think well of its services so VOCA would continue as a client. And having as an insider at VOCA a former employee, someone who was already familiar with our account, made the firm's work here just that much easier.

BECOMING PROFICIENT

In order to become financially literate, I first had to admit and even "celebrate" my ignorance before I could begin learning. I also had to practice my newly acquired skills on a daily basis, with regular feedback, until he and I were comfortable with my performance. You have to be comfortable with your vulnerability in order to learn. Never try to bluff by acting like you understand something you really don't.

The first time I went to a financial seminar–there are many put on by the American Management Association and other organizations–I wanted to wear a bag over my head. The presenters asked the attendees to introduce themselves before the group. I dreaded my turn to make myself vulnerable, to tell everyone I owned a business but knew nothing about finance. To my surprise, I was not the only one. Others taking the seminar, who also had the technical training to own their companies, had as little financial expertise as I did.

Many entrepreneurs are as unsophisticated about financial issues as are many human service managers. What pulls them into business is not their fiscal knowledge but their technical expertise. Entrepreneurial companies are an important part of the American economy–and they are rarely started by accountants. That's why there are so many financial seminars for nonfinancial managers. One of the advantages of attending these management seminars and networking with managers outside our own field is realizing that we're not alone. Our concerns are more typical than they are atypical.

When business owners gather around a table, they generally talk about dollars–profit and loss, debt service, debt-to-equity ratios, borrowings, interest rates–all the contrivances that speak to the bottom line. CEOs of established companies tend to be familiar with that kind of knowledge while CEOs of small, start-up companies are rarely conversant with those terms. In fact, larger companies today are run by people with formal business training. That makes boards of directors and shareholders feel comfortable.

But fiscally astute people don't necessarily make the best human service managers. As CEOs they run into a problem analogous to the problem clinicians have when appointed as heads of agencies: Fiscally trained persons may be adept at handling the books, but they aren't necessarily trained to handle people. So, while human service managers don't need to become experts at money management, we do need to learn how to access information, how to ask the right questions and how to interpret basic financial information.

Learning to prepare a financial statement isn't necessary, but learning to read one is.

In human services, agency heads are rarely picked for their fiscal astuteness except to clean up after a massive crisis. The person who follows an executive director fired for fiscal malfeasance is always there for the short term to fix the fiscal problem. Then the board goes back to hiring the type of person it really wants–an expert in human services.

STRUCTURING AND ACHIEVING BUDGET GOALS

At one point while running VOCA, I met with our controller, who had just given me an intricately detailed analysis of what each of our divisions had to spend, what the revenues were, and what the anticipated expenditures would be. "Let me play a game with you, I said. "I'm going to do a routine called 'A Social Worker Looks at a Budget.'" I then performed a "stand-up comedy monologue" about what appeared to me, in my character of Social Worker, to be the data I was looking at. From what I could ascertain, I was $500,000 in the hole before I even began to spend any money because of the way the information was presented.

As Vince, I understood the analysis–I helped develop it–but I knew my supervisors wouldn't. "They're going to misperceive what all these brackets mean," I told the controller, "and how the numbers are derived. The minute they look at it, they will develop a collective case of butterflies in the stomach. They'll file it under the biggest piles of paperwork in the darkest corners of their offices. They'll say they're going to get to it sometime. They never will."

Actually, budget goals are nothing but company goals expressed in numbers. All organizations have a finite number of resources. However, if a company's employees don't develop an understanding of the financial constraints under which they must operate, they will never meet budget goals, and the company will always be over-budget. Whether the company builds cars or runs human service programs, if it is consistently over budget, it will go broke.

> **Budget goals are nothing but company goals expressed in numbers.**

An agency's fiscal officers are always seen as the bad guys. They are the stingy, secretive people who keep dollars hidden away. They know how foolish and childish we human service people are, so they stash some of our allowance to be doled out as they see fit through the budget year. If that's a description of your fiscal officer, he or she should be fired. That's no way to run a business. Helping supervisors achieve realistic budget goals is a long maturation process to which you must commit your agency early.

Financial information is simply a tool to achieve an agency's goals. It may seem intimidating to those of us with human service backgrounds, but working with money, budgets and numbers is not nearly as difficult as we build it up to be. It's very straightforward. There's no higher math involved; it's all addition, subtraction, multiplication and division, the stuff we learned in grade school. We can do that on our phones.

Simply put, we have a finite number of resources, a finite amount of revenue, and we have to decide how best to use what we have. What are our priorities? How can we spend our dollars most prudently and still leave something in reserve?

The planning procedure does not start with numbers, but rather with the mission of the organization. When you understand your agency's goals and plans, you can then quantify them in dollars to see how they look from a financial standpoint. Managers sometimes try to do it the opposite way. They sit down and write a budget and then try to figure out what their goals and objectives are. That's akin to the tail trying to wag the dog. The financial side should be the last part of a well-planned process.

Many human service executives or program professionals believe that the more dollars they throw into services the better those services are. That's not true. There are other relevant program factors and intangibles. What that belief enables, however, is permission to avoid ranking priorities.

Creating a budget forces people to rank-order what they're doing and examine their effectiveness against the measuring stick of dollars spent.

Helping human service workers understand money is very important yet very difficult. A good way to start is by tying employee bonuses to budgets: Compensate people who efficiently and effectively use dollars better than you compensate people who don't.

We had a program at VOCA we called the VOCA Incentive Plan. Twice each year, we assessed whether we had achieved our quality targets and budget goals. If we had, we presented bonus checks to our non-union employees–not just to managers, but to all of them. This led managers working on budgets to ask, "Do we really need that item? Do we need this expense to do that? I wonder if we could do it another way." They remained as committed to client services as they ever were, but they asked themselves, "Can we get better services for people at lower costs?"

Today's leaders should give thought to offering gain-sharing opportunities to employees as part of their retirement plans. Soon those employees might be checking stock quotes and acting like owners. They'll have the incentive to ask questions about how the organization is performing.

Of course, not all human service organizations can offer

stock participation, a function of being private and publicly traded. Yet other rewards, such as monetary incentives, gain-sharing, promotions, employee recognition, task assignments and other factors can be tied to measurable outcomes and performance and, when they are, it is likely to foster a sense of ownership and commitment.

Obviously, an agency's first priority is to provide good services, and that means employees must spend money. When agency heads or CEOs slam their fists on the table and roar, "We can't continue to spend this way," or "We have to trim back because of budget cuts," they can create fear within the ranks. Then employees spend nothing, which inevitably affects services.

Sometimes managers, out of panic, lack of experience, or inability to see unintended consequences, may come up with solutions that are not well thought out. A while ago, a manager at one of VOCA's homes was charged with cutting costs. He responded by taking away employees' vacation pay. The employees complained, of course, and the problem was eventually solved another way. Yet that can happen if you leave the task to managers who are unprepared.

The key here is to maintain a balance, to teach employees fiscal responsibility and how to balance it with other management considerations. At VOCA people from the finance department teamed up with managers to give them support and helped them work through some of the more technical details of planning their budgets.

Those fiscal people should also be in on program planning. Why? Because they can find out what it costs to provide services, so the budget reflects real costs. Because they can make suggestions as dispassionate third parties and help program staff to prioritize program options. It's the finance department's job to keep an agency solvent. If program staff abrogate their responsibility to set priorities to finance people, they have in effect handed over their programs to the finance department to run. And in many cases, financially trained people know little about program work while program staff know little about finances. If the two sides work together, each becomes cognizant of the other's needs and responsibilities. As the program staff becomes more financially astute, the finance people become more aware of the spirit of the programming. Communication is the key lever and common denominator.

Everything an agency does has a cost, even if the price tag is time. Volunteers do not come free; someone has to train them. Someone has to prepare for a fundraiser. Someone has to prepare the budget. People need to feel at ease with the fact that money is always a consideration and to see dollar issues as accessible rather than threatening.

A good financial officer can help make a budget live for

members of a program staff who don't understand numbers. Along with any presentation to supervisors, he or she
must provide a glossary of financial terms. Those supervisors will be passing on much of the information to their
employees. They need to understand it themselves.

Focus groups can be very useful at budget-planning time,
to test the financial training you provide employees. If the
training works on a focus group, it will likely work with
the general population of your organization. In fact, the
focus group, in concert with your finance manager, can
be used to devise the information package. The worst way
to prepare that information is for the fiscal manager to sit
in his or her office in a vacuum, generating all the numbers, developing the training and devising the explanation. You're better off consulting with the end-users, the
consumers of that information, on what they do and don't
know, and coming up with gentle ways to enable people
to get involved in the process and enjoy it. We all had
subjects in school that we hated. The best teachers were
the ones who took the subjects we thought we hated and
made them fun for us. Our finance managers should be
like those teachers.

When we remain fiscally illiterate, we tend to complain
about what we perceive as the unfeeling, uncaring, bottom-
line privateers and profiteers who are running the world
and lament being victimized by them. Yet unless we take it

upon ourselves to learn how they operate, we will always feel like victims.

MATCHING CLIENT NEEDS TO AVAILABLE FUNDING

We always maintained a non-exclusionary policy at VOCA. We served anyone for whom we had resources. We started the company with the intent to serve the people no one else wanted, the ones with profound disabilities who had fewer options for placement. People with mild challenges–affable, verbal people, were quickly admitted into community programs while those with significant and complicated needs did not receive the same level of attention. So those were the individuals we targeted.

We found, however, that the reimbursement system under which we operated did not take into account the multitude of resources necessary to work with those with greater needs. Although available resources were adequate to provide support for people with mild disabilities, they were not adequate for the needs of people with significant problems, so we took our licks for several months. Then we realized that if we didn't help the funders of our programs understand the need for flexible revenue systems, we would always be in the red and would not be able to serve our target population. Consequently, we became extremely active in helping states develop systems that responded to the varying needs of the people they served. To do that, we had to be able to articulate what that meant in dollars-and-cents terms.

We developed a funding model that let us plot out clients' needs against our costs to serve those needs. For example, people who had serious medical problems required extra nursing hours and medical supplies. Assuming a generically trained staff person would normally attend to a "healthy" client, how much more would we have to pay for a registered nurse or a licensed practical nurse? How much more would we pay for nutritionists trained to handle special diet requirements? How much more would we spend on those special diets? How much would we have to pay for prosthetic devices and ambulation devices? What about speech and hearing consultants? Psychiatrists? Neurologists? The list was never-ending. But as individual person and support plans were developed for each client, we were able to articulate to a reasonable degree what those costs should be and were able to defend them.

A new client's needs are greater, especially after a long stay in an institution, than they are after the client has become acclimated to his or her new surroundings. Clearly, clients who have deteriorating neurological conditions will lose ground. But more often than not, they come in with behavioral anomalies caused by lengthy institutionalization. We were frequently able to ameliorate those problems over a period of time, and in many instances, we even reduced the staff and money necessitated by those problems. There's no better way to curry favor with funders than by asking them to reduce allocations made if you don't require all the money to meet quality service goals. If you try to procure as much as you can, you risk an adversarial relationship with funders, who may decrease your requests if they assume they are inflated.

Most funding systems don't encourage fiscal responsibility. Generally, unless you spend an entire year's allocation, whether or not you actually need all the funds, you will receive less money the following year. Funders don't take into consideration the changing demographics of your client base. Say you happen to have clients move on to less restrictive environments and replace them with clients whose needs are greater. Your funding base for the year has already been predicated on serving people with fewer needs. Since that funding base will not be reconsidered for another year, you lose money.

It would make more sense for funders to develop rate-setting systems that are adjusted periodically, predicated on the changing demographics of the client population a particular agency serves. However, changing the system requires understanding and dialogue, not to mention time and a cooperative political climate.

Many of VOCA's clients from state institutions came to us on high dosages of medication, typically psychotropics. We had been successful in gradually reducing medications, in some instances to zero, and substituting effective behavioral programs for the chemical controls that were previously used to keep them passive. That took knowledgeable professionals, coupled with highly trained direct support professionals, able to supervise the treatment. And those professionals were–and are–expensive.

In the long run, such active engagement saves money, but the up-front expenses are greater. Funders need to know that. As agency executives, we have to put those funders in our shoes–with a shoehorn if necessary–to help them understand the realities of our situations. It's hard to do. But it's not as hard if we've already developed good relationships with senior executives in government.

When we articulate our specific needs to state agencies, they in turn can explain the value of the dollars they request for human services to legislators. Those dollars are then deemed to be tied to individual service criteria. Legislators are more understanding of requests earmarked for meeting specific needs of specific people than they are of generic increases linked somehow to inflation or consumer price indexes. If they are unable or unwilling to support the level of services required to integrate people with profound disabilities into the community, at least they understand the choice they've made. And they are the ones who must bear the consequences, not us.

Don't be afraid to say no to serving people for whom you have inadequate resources. If you try to serve them, you cheat not only those clients, but also your agency. You also let your funders think you're able to do more with less. You can only cut back so much. The cost of services is high, and those expenses will continue to increase as people with more and more disabilities require more and more services.

The irony is that as citizens we want more services but lower taxes. How can we reconcile that? We can't. In the history of the world, people have never expected more from government than they do today. Yet our political milieu includes people who say we're spending too much and all kinds of fiscal restraint legislation measures are on the table.

Usually, there is waste to be trimmed, true. But it's also true that there is never enough to eat at the banquet table. However, the best politicians recognize that only the fat can be trimmed, that the sinew, bone and organ systems must be left intact and maintained in order to provide quality services. That, of course, assumes they know the difference between fat and sinew.

Those of us in human services, who know the effect poor services have on the general public, need to be the conscience of legislatures and funders. We have to demand more for the people we serve. We understand there's not enough money to serve everybody, but let's make sure the people we do serve receive adequate support. We obviously understand that we are living in a world where there are issues that compete with human services that legislators must balance, such as pension obligations, education and the wider world of health care. Still, we must wrestle with our priorities.

Exactly whom should we serve? How do we decide, for example, between homeless people and people with cerebral palsy? Does it make sense to help a person become employable by providing him or her with a prosthetic device, or should the equivalent amount of money go toward helping a person with mental illness? I don't know the answer. Both are human beings. We would all love to say that makes them equally worthy. These are tough issues.

As political winds ebb and flow and demographics change, it becomes harder to predict what tax and other dollars may be available in the future. Human service managers, who are able to defend the real value of their work, will have a leg up dealing with realities as they evolve.

ESTABLISHING AND MAINTAINING SOLID
BANKING RELATIONSHIPS

While businesses and the banking community may sometimes be seen as adversaries, a partnership relationship is preferable. The approach VOCA took in getting to know our lenders mirrored our approach with our finance people. Early on, we professed our ignorance and brought our bankers in as partners to the decision-making process. We wanted them to help us evaluate how much money we would need not only to survive but to grow. In turn, we had to help them understand why we needed the money to begin with. In wooing lending institutions, we made it a point to get to the highest echelons possible, knowing the real decisions are made behind closed doors by people one never sees in the lobby. It's up to a company's chief executives to be sure that the story told behind those doors is the story as it truly exists. Loan officers may be convinced that a loan request is worthy, but if their ability to sell their superiors on it is faulty, the loan will not be approved.

Many bankers are uncomfortable dealing with human services. As we've seen our economy evolve from brick and mortar stores and factories to online retail, healthcare and service companies, banking has evolved as well. Most likely, bankers are providing loans to organizations they might not have done business with 20 years ago. And human service companies remain a challenge. One banker told me that lending to a human service agency is like lending to a church; how do you foreclose on a group home for people with intellectual disabilities and put those people out on the street? You need to be able to articulate to bankers in very real terms how the services you provide generate revenue, how historically, under every administration, money has always been available for services such as yours. If you can't sell that, you're unbankable.

Successful banking is based on relationships. It's based on credibility and trust. A bank's decision-makers want to feel confident that what you tell them is true, that when you say you can do something, you actually can. That's probably as important, if not more so, than the financial details those decision-makers analyze as part of the lending process. It takes time to cultivate that kind of relationship. It requires keeping your bankers up-to-date on what you're doing. It requires telling them right away if things turn out different from what you anticipated. Don't let them find out on their own.

Assume your lenders will talk among themselves. When you go to a bank for $20,000, give the loan officer the name of the guy who previously lent you $10,000. You might as well offer the information; the bank will check your credit anyway. And make sure your personal credit is impeccable. If you can't take care of your own finances, the bank will assume you can't take care of the company's.

It also doesn't hurt to have your personal accounts at the bank you borrow from. We brought our bankers into VOCA's corporate offices to tell our employees what they could offer in terms of personal services. We didn't ask our employees to move their accounts, but some did and the bank picked up 15 or 20 customers among the 60 people at our corporate headquarters. They helped us, so we helped them as we could.

You should also give thought to which bank you choose. Community banks are currently less common as the large national chains open branches everywhere. Still, you may be more able to develop a meaningful relationship with a smaller entity where you have a better chance of working with top executives. At the same time, it's no longer safe to assume that every bank will remain in business indefinitely. As you evaluate which bank you want to do business with, ask for annualized financial statements, or check with a credit reporting service. There are several that specialize in financial institutions.

As we at VOCA got better at doing our job, our bankers helped us celebrate the results. They came to our homes where they met and ate dinner with our residents. They saw, heard, tasted and smelled our services. They also obtained affirmations about our services from state regulators. They understood our business more than they possibly could have from reading our profit-and-loss statements, our monthly financials, and our quarterly reports. It took time to make that relationship work. But it made our bankers understand why, with their limited resources, we might have been more loan-worthy than another organization. For our part, we never failed to pay a debt back on time. Sometimes that was easier said than done, but we made that commitment and kept it.

ASSETS AND DEBT

Debt-to-equity ratio is one of the analytical measures bankers look at when judging how risky a loan might be. The more debt your company has, the more risky it is, and the more risky a loan would be. So one goal in your planning should be to maintain the company's debt within certain limits. You can define those limits internally and work with your bankers to help determine what your financial policies should be.

We typically think of equity as home equity, the difference between what a house costs at the time it was built or bought and what it could be sold for now. When bankers offer you a line of credit secured by your home equity, they look at the worst-case scenario, the smallest profit likely if the house had to be sold in order to repay your debt. You pledge your house in return for that line of credit. If you are unable to repay your loan, the bank seizes and resells your house to recoup its money.

You may not think of your agency as having equity, but it simply has equity of a different kind. Although your receivables are not equity, they are security. If they are tied to ongoing funding, so much the better. Your building may have equity in it, and so may any inventory you have. The best asset of all is net cash on hand because you can use it to capitalize new growth rather than continually depending on borrowing. And when you do ask for money, the bank will look kindly on your ability to handle funds.

As always, the best advice is to manage your money well, invest wisely and get the best returns. The bank wants to know that you're using the funds you have in the most responsible way possible, that you're neither overpaying nor underpaying your employees, for example, but are compensating them at market value. The bank wants to know that you're adequately insured. It wants to know that your services are considered worthy by funders, that a need for such services has been articulated over time, and that such services have historically been funded and will continue to be funded. A need for your services makes you bankable even though you don't have a warehouse full of equipment you can sell. It's your job to redefine debt-to-equity ratios for your bankers, to present necessary services instead of durable goods.

It's the bank's job, on the other hand, to watch for danger signs–and the signs it looks for are recession and inflation. Many human service businesses are recession and inflation proof; the need for their services is inversely proportional to bad news in the economy. If that applies to you, help your bankers understand it. It makes you more bankable.

If payment for your services is pegged to an inflation factor, that is, if your increases in revenue are tied not only to greater numbers of people served but to fluctuations in a consumer price index, tell your bankers. They will feel much more comfortable knowing your funding sources make adjustments to counter inflation.

MEASUREMENT MAKES A DIFFERENCE

One of the most important things you need to do involves measurement. Measurement, and the resulting data, provides the foundation for planning, reimbursement, how funders see you, how you frame your political case, your quality efforts, and more. Valid statistical analyses will provide you an invaluable tool to monitor your results and demonstrate the value of the services your agency is delivering. Today, some organizations are utilizing dashboard approaches to track their key performance indicators.

Based on the size and scope of your organization, whether in terms of the number of people served, budget or employee headcount, the metrics you employ may be different, but the essential matter of paying attention to results remains the same. You also need to collect the data that is important to you from a quality management perspective.

You most likely will need to secure the services of a professional, who will be able to translate what you want to measure into understandable data. The key word is "understandable." The data you measure must be understood by a wide variety of data users.

Some organizations may have the necessary staff expertise to create the data tracking systems required. There are also a number of software programs currently available that can be purchased and employed fairly easily with a degree of customization.

One approach that may be useful is to develop a group of funders and potential clients who can provide feedback as to the utility of your quality measures. You need to make sure this focus group is run in a safe environment that engenders unbiased feedback. Ask them if your data points are understandable and which data points they use in making decisions. Once you have assessed the data that have the greatest impact on decision-making, begin collecting and prioritizing that information.

What do you measure? Remember that the standard is, "Are your clients better off after they received your services than before they engaged with you?" So you are measuring client outcomes, such as new abilities and life skills that benefit the individual. The more objective the measures, the better. Setting specific goals about specific behaviors, and measuring against those goals, provides feedback to the individual and a gauge of the work that still needs to be done. In addition, tracking your measurements over time will provide insights on the lasting effects of your services.

Ask yourself, why clients and those who fund you seek out your services as opposed to the myriad other services and choices available to them? Why should funders, both public and private, support your program more or less than some other agency?

No agency I know is satisfied with its level of funding. Dollars for human services tend to be last on the list of public funding priorities. Politicians are constantly running for re-election on reducing costs rather than increasing them. Even private foundations and donors are concerned that their funds are being wisely spent. The data you have collected will go a long way to help all your financial supporters understand why your agency programs should be sustained and even expanded. The message should be clear: adequate quality service delivery will save money in the long-run. Investing in programs that foster client independence that can be proven is just good business and good stewardship of public and private funds.

The challenge is to document how your consumer's lives have changed because of the services they received, both now and over time. Aside from self-reporting their progress, your clients need to have demonstrated measurable competencies that help them lead more productive lives. These changes should be recognized and reported by the environments within which they function. Increased client functionality is the business of your business and the ultimate goal of every human service organization. It is its raison d'etre.

THE POLITICS OF REIMBURSEMENT

Government has a greater impact on what happens in health and human services than does any other entity. Through programs, such as Medicare and Medicaid, government dominates every sector of the market. Whether it's state or federal government, each has myriad bureaucrats and departments, all with their own agendas. And then there are the legislative bodies, whose agendas may conflict with everybody else's.

Obviously, one of the first steps in receiving reimbursements is to make sure the funding agency is satisfied with the services it's buying. What do people want out of a program? What type of service delivery do they want? Do the various governmental entities see your services as necessary, valuable and good quality? If you can convince people that you're performing a necessary and valuable service, you're more likely to convince them that it's worth their while to pay a reasonable price for the services you provide.

Working with government takes tremendous patience. Instead of working with a single entity, such as a bank and a single focal point, you are working with a multilayered bureaucracy in which you may have to wade through dozens of tiers, a variety of departments, and multiple, conflicting interactions and interests.

You have to deal with each administrative office separately. You have to deal with each state separately. You have to negotiate your way between the people administering funding programs and legislators to ensure that adequate funds are appropriated, and you may be dealing with county government, state entities and federal agencies as well. You will have to deal with the various surveyors, who audit the quality of your programming and your record-keeping, to maintain your licenses and certification. And the surveyors typically want to see documentation that bears no relationship either to what you're being paid to do or to the amount of resources you have. You may have one government department telling you what to do to maintain your licenses and another saying it won't reimburse you if you do. You need to be able to work through such issues and articulate to government officials that everything you do carries a price tag, and somebody has to pay.

The bureaucracy will get only more entangled. The number of government departments and agencies involved in health care continues to increase. Each new face on the scene piles more regulations on top of the ones that already exist. Each new regulation adds to the already immense piles of paperwork required of us. And as government agencies tighten their belts, they continuously want us to do more as they pay less. Managed care, with its own models of funding and service options, adds even more complexity to the task.

That's why it's so important to be politically active. If you can work your way inside the bureaucracy and develop a trusting relationship with the person who heads it–the governor, the mayor, whomever–you can be a catalyst for change. Yelling and screaming about how bad a problem is provides no solution. You need to be a trusted ally before you will be allowed to tinker with the bureaucratic fiber.

Many newly elected officials are amazed at how intransigent the bureaucracy really is. In truth, government is not run by elected officials but by civil servants who have been on the job forever and will retire from their positions. They are the ones who know the codes. They are the ones who push the buttons on the computer to cut checks for services. Many of those people survive only by perpetuating the bureaucracy. They have a disincentive to clean up the system because that would mean loss of jobs, possibly their own.

At one time, the governor of Ohio asked me to head a task force of agency executives and consumers to go over the multiplicity of regulations we follow. How many are duplicated? How many of those duplicated regulations can be eliminated and still keep up the level of quality government has to maintain? The answers to those questions are complex. Elected officials have the authority to make changes. Politicians, who actually take that risk, must be able to trust that the people they've assigned to do it for them won't strip away the safeguards that have to be there to ensure that the public is not ripped off.

Appropriate, well-executed regulations do protect the people we serve. You'd better hope, for instance, that the steak, eggs, tomato or tuna you eat for dinner tonight has passed some kind of regulatory inspection. To have no regulations at all would create chaos. We would have no way of knowing that we could safely drink tap water or that the cans we opened were free of deadly bacteria. But, if regulations develop lives unto themselves and do nothing to improve service quality, they need to be changed or eliminated. The private sector must demand of government–not as accuser but as partner–that those regulations be reviewed. We're all in this together. Let's see if there's a better way.

FUNDRAISING IN THE NOT-FOR-PROFIT SECTOR

Raising money is more than having a bake sale on the corner. It's an art. The public, increasingly conservative with its charitable dollars, wants to know why one organization is more deserving of those dollars than the millions of others that are also asking for funding. Clearly, there will be more demands on discretionary giving as more and more organizations ask for a finite number of dollars.

The executive soliciting public money must be able to articulate specific uses for the funds. People tend to give more readily for a specific program as opposed to generic "agency improvement." They demand accountability, especially from an organization they expect to return to them year after year for continued funding. They want to be kept informed of the strides that the organization makes in improving its use of funds. They may even want to have an active role in the planning process. It's a mistake to assume that donors who have funded a particular agency for 10 or 15 years will continue to do so forever. With so many appeals for so few dollars, funders are more likely to give to organizations that see them as partners rather than as giving machines.

As an executive, you must be willing and ready to make public how your agency uses the money it has. There are a lot of scams out there, a lot of scurrilous organizations that allegedly represent veterans or people with disabilities or some other group considered "worthy." If you are on the up-and-up, especially if you are seeking funding for the first time, you need to assess how to present your agency as deserving. It takes good public relations and open, honest disclosure.

It takes good public relations and open, honest disclosure to present your agency as deserving.

Third-party endorsements may also be useful. If you can present a prospective donor with a portfolio of endorsements, that donor has reason to believe that "Yes, I am giving my money to a group of people who deserve it."

There are a wide range of additional methods you can use to raise funds, particularly if you are a not-for-profit or have a related organization that has received not-for-profit status from the Internal Revenue Service, allowing donors to deduct charitable giving. You may also want to keep abreast of changing tax laws that might affect who can deduct what and how much. Some organizations hold an annual appeal that asks people and businesses to pledge at various levels for the coming year. The appeal can be complete with an event, such as a gala or golf outing.

You may want to recruit a fundraising auxiliary board, made up of volunteers who have relatives in your homes or are interested in your cause. They can do the organizing and logistics and may decide the event will honor someone well known, who will then recruit friends and associates to "buy" tables at the gala dinner. The volunteers might also approach businesses for contributions to a "silent auction," where attendees can bid far more than the items are actually worth or do other fundraising activities. Such an auxiliary has the added benefit of creating strong community bonds for your organization.

Another method of raising money is through legacy giving. You will probably need to work with an accountant or actuary to develop instruments through which people may leave bequests when they pass away or put funds into an instrument that pays them interest or retirement income while funding your agency.

You will also want to explore foundation grants and bequests. There are online sites and organizations that categorize donor organizations and provide application requirements. Depending on the size of your agency, you may want to recruit an employee with grant-writing expertise, who can spend a large portion of time in this endeavor. In some areas, there are also civic groups that bring together philanthropic entities, potential grant recipients, and others that can be useful.

Nowadays we live in an environment of constant ratings. Almost every time we make a purchase online, we are asked to rate both the product and the seller. There are a variety of sites, such as the consumer site Yelp, and more specialized sites rating charities and agencies. While many of these are aimed at users of your services, they are also visible to potential employees and funders. You need to monitor any comments about your organization. There are services, such as Google alerts and other methods, that can help you do so. In addition, old-line organizations, such as the Better Business Bureau, can vouch for you as a legitimate fundraising organization.

Through all of these activities, you, as the executive, also have to act the part. An agency's ability to raise funds can be damaged if its executives are perceived to flaunt wealth or privilege, or be unworthy in other ways.

Professionals know the techniques that work. They may also have access to additional lists of people who give and are likely to give. They know how to approach people, what kinds of brochures to do, and how to run media campaigns. Fundraising is a profession like any other; it takes time to learn. A good fundraiser can articulate your agency's goals and package them attractively. It's a great way to sell your organization to the public.

If you do decide to use outside help, you may want to call

other agencies or nonprofits for recommendations. Be sure to check references and any online reviews before you proceed. When you interview the person or company, look for an understanding of what you are and what you do. Talented fund-raisers will become valuable partners in building your funds-worthy case. Remember that funding is only half of the equation. You need to be a good steward of the support you get, and financial competence is key to that ability.

Making a Positive
Community Impact

8

ESTABLISHING AND ENHANCING
COMMUNITY RELATIONSHIPS

Since most human service agencies are supported with
tax money, it is essential to our survival that the public
perceive our services as necessary. But most people in the
community don't understand the relevance of those services until they or someone in their family needs them. It
is up to us as agencies to shape what we do in such a way
that people, who have not been personally touched by the
issues we address, understand the worth of our services
to the society at large.

This is not an easy task, especially in view of trends that
include families living at great distances from each other
and the use of electronic devices to communicate in almost
every societal sphere. In addition, many people operate out
of a scarcity model that defines helping someone else as

short-changing themselves. It is up to us to help foster the empathy, sympathy and understanding of connectedness that will cast us in a positive community light.

Most people, going about their daily lives, are unaware of the physical infrastructure around them, let alone the presence of people with disabilities. However, when a jagged pothole punctures their tire, they want to know who is responsible, something that may lead them to understand that road maintenance takes a predictable level of funding. By the same token, the need for human services is also an ongoing reality. So an important part of an agency's role is not only to show that the money we have is being used appropriately, but also to educate the general public as to why our services are needed.

As an executive in a human service agency, consider yourself an ambassador and educator. Your very presence can play a role in familiarizing people with what you do and emphasizing its necessity. You can make a greater impact if you take an active role in your community–join the chamber of commerce and service groups, attend local government meetings, be present in local discussions about education and other topics, join a local board and sponsor community entities, such as Little League teams or events. People will come to know you and, by extension, your

> **As an executive in a social service agency, consider yourself an ambassador and an educator.**

agency. They will be more open to your needs as they come to understand them by spending time with you.

As to more formal efforts, few agencies spend any time or money on general public education. That can be a mistake. What if you prepared a talk, for example, that laid out population level statistics, the cost to society and the community of doing nothing, and how that cost is lessened because of what you do. Pepper the talk with a few poignant stories of actual clients and their families–you don't have to use their real names unless they want you to–and offer to present the talk at civic organizations, service clubs and libraries. Many organizations are always looking for speakers, and you could help your agency at the same time you build good will.

Of course, to prepare such a talk, you need to be aware of how satisfied your clients are with the services they receive, a fact you should be aware of anyway. When an agency executive is asked, "How do you know whether or not you're doing any good?" the answer should be, "Here are data that show people are better off because of our services than they were before they came to us. We have made a positive change in people's lives."

Growth data are a reliable way of presenting that information, given the importance of confidentiality and anonymity in our field. But you might be surprised at how many people are willing to come forward and talk about their personal experiences with your agency. You won't know unless you ask them.

When former clients come to you and say, "I can't thank you enough. This is the finest thing I've ever been through. You're wonderful," they might be willing to acknowledge you publicly. You could ask them questions, such as:

- ■ "Would you tell your story on social media?"
- ■ "Would you rate us on a ratings site?"
- ■ "Can we write about you on our blog?"
- ■ "Can we feature you on our website?"
- ■ "Would you write a letter?"
- ■ "Would you let us do a piece about you in the newspaper?"

My experience has been, more often than not, that people are happy to do so. They genuinely appreciate the quality of services they have received and the impact it has had on their lives. Seeing satisfied customers creates a certain aura in the public around what you do. Folks may not be excited at the thought of paying taxes, but they're glad to see their money used to good ends.

As we compete for the ever-shrinking dollars available to us, we have to become more creative about selling what we do. It is part of our professional responsibility. We must not think of selling and marketing as distasteful, but as the necessary underpinning that supports our work, our jobs and the services the community needs.

RELATING TO THE MEDIA

People receive news and information today through many sources, including social media, websites, cable news and friends. The "traditional" media–broadcast networks, magazines and newspapers–are still around although, outside of a couple of well subsidized print publications, many are struggling to survive.

Other factors influence our relationships with media as well. For one thing, the digital age has ushered in a world in which many people receive their updates from sources they already agree with, thus reinforcing their existing beliefs. At the same time, particularly with younger people, attention spans are shorter than ever. For instance, as a teenager, my son used to watch movies in two-minute increments. While he might have been a bit more drastic than most, there is no doubt that the digitization of everything continues to change how we think.

Not only do people derive their impressions of what's going on in the world in 30-second sound bites, they make up their minds about something by the way it makes them feel. While current research in neuroscience and areas, such as behavioral economics, are teaching us that our emotions and biases often overtake our logic, some people may find it counterintuitive while others, such as those in advertising, have long recognized its importance. In addition, more people than ever are influenced by what their friends and trusted sources recommend, rather than relying on their independent judgment.

Dealing with these changes can pose challenges, but they present new opportunities as well. To begin with, there are more vehicles than ever before that offer us opportunities to talk about our work. For instance, you probably have an agency website, Facebook page and blog. If you don't have these, set them up.

Facebook and other social media sites allow you to write about your agency while they allow others to write about you. The benefits of these sites can outweigh any potential of negative posting, but they do need to be monitored. If someone wants to say something negative about your agency, they have a variety of outlets–and if that happens, you probably want to call in a crisis management professional.

Other forms of media you may want to consider using are:

1. *Twitter:* You can tweet about events, (e.g., fundraising events), milestones (e.g., an agency anniversary), and information (e.g., an article written about human services) that can help your community better understand human service issues. You can encourage people in the community to sign up for your Twitter feed.

2. *Common interest and support group sites:* These sites provide clients and their relatives a safe place to talk confidentially with people going through similar situations. You might consider hosting or sponsoring such a site.

3. *Local newspapers and media:* Depending on your location, local community newspapers seem more viable than big city dailies. They are sustained by local sports and real estate, and many of them publish a variety of stories of local interest.

4. *Specialty trade magazines:* These publications still exist along with their websites. If they, or any other media write about you, you can make reprints and send them out, take screenshots and post them on your website, and hand them out if you are speaking. You can send a tweet message referencing it. Anytime there is coverage of any sort, you can multiply its value.

Every agency needs an active public relations plan to take advantage of these and other publicity opportunities. While PR can be expensive and its results are not always trackable in the moment, it is worth it.

Some human service agency executives may erroneously believe that less media coverage is the best media coverage because reporters typically want to find fault with us rather than tell the good side of our story. This is not necessarily true and may be an impression created when there is news coverage of institutional malfeasance. Knowing that investigative reporters are the folks who search out news as opposed to writing features or human interest stories, we at VOCA identified those who were assigned to cover human service issues in their community. We called them and invited them to meet us and look at the services we were providing. In almost every instance, because we had initiated the contact, we were able to develop positive relationships that served us well when a crisis inevitably occurred. We helped these reporters understand the nature of our work with all the difficulties and triumphs we encountered as we served the individuals entrusted to our care. We recounted stories about individual client achievements, which worked well to personalize what we were doing. Many times, these reporters elected to do a positive piece on our services that enhanced the public's perception of who we were and why we chose to do what we did.

Since media has changed in recent years, regional and local news organizations are operating with scarcer resources, and there may be fewer investigative or "beat" reporters covering human services. Reporters that do exist are overworked, and, outside of a few major markets, are most likely called on to cover several different areas, offering them little opportunity to develop expertise on any given area. However, if you call the general reporters in your local media and let them know who you are, you will begin to build a relationship. And because they're so busy, they may be open to stories you suggest about something you'd like to highlight.

The media, however, goes far beyond the news into feature stories, documentaries, how-to-do-its, and other types of coverage. The need for "content," as it is sometimes known, is great, and many outlets are looking for "supplied" material that they don't have to pay for. In addition, many independent writers are creating specialty blogs, podcasts and other instruments that need material. All of them need what you can supply.

In order to capitalize on these opportunities, you need to be good at regularly telling about your company or agency in a way that makes people listen. You, or your PR firm, need to research and cultivate these outlets. Try a Google search or look at the publications and sites that YOU regularly read.

You must publicly celebrate the quality of your services on a regular basis. To do this, put your plan in place and cultivate relationships before they are needed. Get to know any reporters from your local media and tell them about your

> **Make it one of your goals to celebrate the quality of your services publicly on a regular basis.**

services. Provide them with electronic fact sheets, descriptions of programs, proper descriptive terminology, funding descriptions where feasible and overviews of your agency that they can easily reference. In developing a relationship with a reporter, you must show him or her why you are so passionate about your cause by communicating it in a way that is emotionally engaging. Passion is contagious.

One way to disseminate information that might be available if you still have an independent TV station in your market is the Public Service Announcement or PSA. PSA's grew in an era when most TV came through regulated broadcast networks. These were required to offer airwave access to entities that were not-for-profit or otherwise supporting the public good. If you have such a station in your market–and they are scarce since most independent stations have been bought up by syndicates and large companies–check with them as to their requirements. You may be able to submit notices of events you're holding.

Another way of publicizing your events may be to think about it in a different way. Perhaps the clients themselves are doing something unusual to raise the funds, such as having a sale of craft items they make themselves. That could make a good human interest feature for a local station, although, be warned, you will probably have competition. You will need to call the assignment editor of the local station and let him or her know how visually interesting the making and selling of the crafts are, how dedicated your residents are to their art, and what they're trying to achieve.

You have to be enthusiastic about your program and seek publicity for it. If you serve people with developmental disabilities, there are wonderful stories every day of people learning new skills and developing new assimilation techniques that allow them to participate in the community. At VOCA, we celebrated the assimilation of our clients into the community by highlighting the efforts they made in helping other people and their successes at work. It earned us a lot of positive press.

For example, a resident of ours was picked as McDonald's Employee of the Year for the Columbus, Ohio region. He went to Minneapolis to receive an award. Since McDonald's already had an active program of hiring people with disabilities, we pointed out the PR possibilities for their company, as well as for us. Fortunately, McDonald's administrators agreed, and they successfully pitched the story to the press. If you investigate your area, you might discover other companies with whom you are in contact that are concerned about their community image.

One thing to remember in building a relationship with the press is that reporters do not want to be duped. So the way to get to know them and gain their trust is to always tell them the truth. Let them know what you're doing, and if they're honest and forthright, as most of them are, they'll give you an even shot.

A final note: The PR goal of an agency supporting the populations we serve is to help people understand how they are personally affected by the situations of others. Sometimes there is a tendency for the public to "blame" disadvantaged people for their problems. Those with addictions often fall into this category. However, the growing opioid epidemic demands that we initiate a public conversation, highlighting the causes and viable methods of addressing the problem.

Obviously, media and internet outlets can be important partners. Our part is to make writers, producers, bloggers and others understand our story and why it needs to be told. Most people in the media see themselves as public servants and are more than happy to help deliver an important message. Sometimes they can even help us develop the best tactic for getting the point across. That's why they're in business.

THE MANAGER AS IMAGE-MAKER

Nowadays the average tech employee may be wearing jeans, shorts, sandals or any manner of comfortable looking outfits, so you may not believe it, but years ago, IBM mandated that all their service people wear white shirts and dark ties and carry their tools in attaché cases. While people laughed at the time, they did carry a message of professionalism and confidence. We still see the more formal attire used for the same reasons when we go into a large law firm or a bank.

In the same way, we need to pay attention to the image our executives and employees convey. Just as you feel more confident if your doctor or dentist is wearing scrubs, there is a certain degree of professionalism that our clients deserve.

In these days of "business casual" dress, deciding what is "professional" can be tricky. And you may be reluctant to institute a dress code when you never had one before. But well-dressed employees have and convey a sense of confidence. For many people, dressing differently than they might while just lounging about at home, helps them prepare themselves for work.

There may also be practical considerations depending on an employee's duties. In many situations, for example, open-toed shoes or sandals may not be safe. So invite your people to take a look at their colleagues and ask themselves whether they would feel confident in the services offered if they had a problem serious enough to seek help from your agency.

PLANNING

The continued survival of your agency is going to depend on management's ability to predict future social needs and plan strategies to meet them. Managers don't have the luxury of involving themselves myopically in today's crises. Those who can't allow themselves the creative free time for long-range planning will suffer immeasurably from that lack of foresight-and so will their agencies. I started in this business working for some of those agencies that no longer exist because of their failure to plan. They also failed to tell anybody why the services they provided needed to be sustained.

No matter how important you think your work is today, tomorrow it might be considered frivolous or useless by the people who make decisions about your funding. Fear is a great motivator. If you're afraid your agency might not exist in a few years, you should be motivated to do some strategic planning.

> **If you're afraid your agency might not exist in a few years, you should be motivated to do some strategic planning.**

Typically, however, we human service managers become caught in the quagmire of day-to-day realities. Unfortunately, we often lack the skills and experience to plan for the future. Strategic planning requires setting aside uninterrupted time to look at where you are regularly throughout the year, where you need to be, and what you need to do to get there. Assessing where you are now assumes that you have studied the variables that brought you to this place. Deciding where you're going means that, predicated on the history and projections of demographic data, you can forecast future needs, how you and your agency will respond to those needs, and what infrastructure changes need to be made to ready your agency to meet those future needs.

At VOCA, we found it beneficial to have consultants help us ask some of the questions we were hesitant to ask ourselves, to challenge our decisions and hypotheses about the need for our services. That's an uncomfortable process to go through. Nobody takes to change easily.

The way you do business today, the hierarchy of employees you have, may be antithetical to meeting the challenges of the future. New challenges generally beget organizational design changes. An organization mutates to fit a new environment that requires new services. Ironically, many managers know that intellectually, but the way they operate is to expect the system to change for their organizations. The decision to take on new opportunities or new business revolves around the question, "Does it fit the way we are?" rather than, "Do we fit the way it is?" Again, the cell phone industry is a good example. Motorola and Nokia made better cell phones; Apple changed what cell phones are.

We in human services need to be sure we are not doing the same thing better, but are doing our best to ascertain how human services may change. Every management journal is replete with exhortations to be evolving continuously. Unfortunately, most human service managers don't read them. We need to.

The need for human services is likely to grow as the 21st century unfolds. This means that agencies such as ours are already targets for take-over by large corporations. Business goes where the revenue is, and revenue will be generated out of our industry. What will our role be in making that happen? If we don't lead the way, others will. And those others may not have the values and ethics that we have. If we are truly client-centered and customer-centered, if we believe in the self-determination of the people we serve, we must be responsible for developing a service structure that can meet the needs of individuals in the most efficient way possible. And we must reassure the public that we are the ones to meet those needs.

MARKETING

Marketing and selling are two separate functions. You market your services to your intended clients by delineating how your service is different from your competition. Remember, you are competing both for people who will use your services and also for funding. There are several steps you need to take to accomplish this.

One of the first is to develop a professionally designed website. Your website should be upbeat and inviting. It should include descriptive, positive success stories about the people you serve; testimonials from clients, relatives, funders and your community, as well as clear descriptions of your organization and services. You might include notices of community events and invitations to celebrate milestones. It should talk about your staff and, if appropriate, encourage people to contribute and volunteer.

We have talked about outcomes, and they can be qualities that differentiate you from other providers. For example, data, such as how a number of your clients have achieved levels of independence as a result of your services, will solidify the impressions you convey in your stories.

Your website is just the beginning of your digital presence. You need to have active social media pages beginning with Facebook but potentially on other sites, providing people the chance to interact with you and your staff.

You also need to be active in your community, becoming involved with service clubs like Kiwanis, Rotary and Elks. These groups are also always looking for speakers. When we offered to speak, we were constantly surprised at how little the general public knew about what we did and the value we brought to the community.

If you are unsure of your public speaking skills, joining Toastmasters International is an excellent way to gain confidence through regular practice in a safe environment. If you don't have a Toastmaster's chapter near you, enroll in one of the many public speaking courses offered by local colleges, universities and community colleges. Being able to express yourself both verbally and in writing is essential to your success.

The more information the public has about what we do, the better informed they will be and the better the chances are of their endorsing the expenditure of funds to support our people with disabilities and our services. Lack of information produces complacency at best and hostility at worst.

SELLING

Every business, including yours, is constantly selling the value their services bring to clients. You "sell" every day. Whether you're selling your partner on the value of making a purchase, selling your child on the consequences of not doing their homework, or asking your employer for a raise, we are constantly selling to everyone. Many human service professionals think they are not comfortable with selling, but many times they have to "sell" the people they serve on the importance of changing their behaviors–which is the toughest sale of all. So commit to learning how to sell the value of your services.

Selling in our field occurs in one-to-one personal encounters when people are making a decision to use or fund our services. No one would ever be expected to be hired by a company they had not researched. Any successful prospective employee understands that a successful interview process requires the applicant to sell him or herself to the prospective employer. If you have researched what these people want and what they are willing to pay for, you will be better prepared to match what your services offer to a demonstrated need. If, on the other hand, your services are not current and fail to meet the needs of your customers, you will eventually fail.

The point is that if we do our homework, know what our stakeholders want, understand the necessary costs of providing our services, and demonstrate that we are good stewards of the funds we receive, we can flourish in today's competitive human service environment.

Focus on Continuous Improvement

The day we were born, we began hearing an important piece of advice from our parents. They began to teach us that we should never be satisfied with the person we are right now; there's always room for development. The parent who said, "I know you worked hard to get that B, but I know you can get an A next time," gave us the message that whatever we do can be improved.

As VOCA grew and evolved over the years, one of the hardest things for me was that I continued to be embarrassed by some of the decisions I made early on. When I think back on the ramifications of some of the choices I made, I wonder who made those ridiculous decisions. I truly am different now than I was then, in ways that I would never have expected. My substance is the same, but my knowledge has grown. I often said that, had I applied for the job of CEO of VOCA, I would not have been hired. I was ill-prepared for what the company was. But I was fearful enough of failing that I continued to grow as the company grew. It was an agonizing process.

It is inevitable that, as a manager, you're going to screw up. You have to learn to deal with that in your heart of hearts, to neither beat yourself up for it nor allow anyone else to do so. You can do that more easily if you think of yourself as an ever-evolving individual, recognizing that it is the nature of humans to change. If you come to believe, "Now I have arrived. Now I'm ready to kick back," you will surely be disappointed. The truth is, you never do "arrive," so don't be surprised to find yourself never kicking back.

In a healthy organization, you continue to improve as you listen to the people around you. When you improve yourself, your company or agency can't help improving as well, because the impetus for your enrichment will be healthy employees who enjoy their jobs, who work in a well-managed atmosphere, and who themselves are continuously improving. Such an atmosphere draws people, rather than cajoles them, to improve. Instead of your having to take the role of parent and say, in effect, "Next time, get that A," you can depend on your employees to tell themselves, "I know I can do A work now because I know so much more than I ever did before."

> **In a healthy organization, you continue to improve when you listen to the people around you.**

It's easier to be more competent when you have more competence. That's obvious. But don't think that you're as competent now as you will be five years from now. If you focus on continuous improvement, you'll be even more competent then.

That's why people are more reluctant to retire early now than they used to be. Many find themselves evolving to peak efficiency in their 60s and 70s. They're healthy people–physically and mentally–who are seeing the results of a lifetime of dedication to continuous personal improvement and are just now hitting their prime.

I know a lot of people who listened to the message that life was over at 65, who stopped working, went home and waited to die. But they were in for a shock. They didn't die. Some of those folks felt cheated. They'd worked very hard, they'd done their job, they'd contributed to society, and now it was time to rest and die. And what happened? They got healthier.

One concept of retirement, which, for a variety of reasons has become less prevalent in recent years, was terrible. It suggested retreating not only from a job but from life itself. What is the significance of a particular age? Rather than retirement age, maybe it's a good time for a person to take all the skills he or she has learned and put them to a new use. I often think of a quote from Satchel Paige, a groundbreaking major league pitcher and Baseball Hall of Famer in 1971, who was known for saying, "How old would you be if you didn't know your age?"

One of our outside directors, who was in his 60s, used to be a very aggressive executive in some major national corporations. With us, he was giving back. He could sit with me and listen as I talked about my innermost feelings and fears, and he understood what I was saying because he'd had those same feelings and fears and grown past them. That's a great gift, the pot of gold at the end of the rainbow of self-actualization.

My friend had been through tremendous pain, both personal and organizational, to get to where he was. He truly paid the price for the big titles he'd carried. But then, as a consultant of his own little company and as a professional board member to a number of other companies, he was able to draw from his experiences and help others profit from them. Finding folks like that is essential for you as a manager. They can provide steppingstones to your own development.

Managers can improve their skills by asking themselves and the people around them periodically, "Why are we doing what we're doing the way we're doing it?" As I visited our homes in different states, I often asked employees I'd never met before, "Why do you do your job that way?" More often than not, they said, "This is the way we've always done it." What a terrible answer. It means that the employee didn't feel responsible for making things better. The fact that we've always done it that way was enough. That person wasn't going to buck the system, wasn't even invested in the system, and just came to work to pull a paycheck.

To think that every employee can come up with wonderful ideas is absurd. But many can, many more than you ever thought. The corollary to, "Why do we do what we do?" is "What might be a better way?" Ask the question, and listen to the answers.

DEVELOPING A MANAGERIAL KNOWLEDGE BASE

Your commitment to management development requires you to know that there is a body of knowledge out there specific to improving managerial skills. Take inventory of what you read, the kinds of seminars and conferences you go to. If your development is not management-oriented, you're kidding yourself.

Chances are you will continue to go to the conferences you went to before you were a manager. All your buddies are there, and they are great times to throw away your management hat and be one of the folks again. There's nothing wrong with that. But you also need to affiliate yourself with people who do what you do now. That's the support system, the networking. You'll be amazed to find that the managers you rub elbows with are all as nervous in their positions as you are, I don't care how long they've been in the business.

I've been to a number of CEO round tables and seminars. At first, when I was invited to go to them, I'd discard those invitations as quickly as they arrived. I was reluctant to join those folks. Those were real company presidents, people with MBAs and accounting degrees, people who knew what they were doing. And who was I? I was a social worker who happened to head a company. If they found out how little I knew about business, they'd laugh me out of the room.

I finally mustered up my courage and went to one of the seminars, promising myself to be as much a part of the wallpaper as possible–which for me is very hard–and not to reveal my weaknesses. Lo and behold, I saw people my age and older with responsible positions in any number of corporate environments talking about how frightened they were, how ill-prepared they were, how little time they had to develop themselves and the problems they were having with their employees. How different from meeting folks at a country club or in some other social atmosphere. There they talked about their companies' successes, and how many points their stocks had gone up. No one's business had ever gone through hard times.

In the seminar environment, everyone felt comfortable sharing their dirty laundry. As I became more comfortable in the group, I began to contribute more, and all my fears left me. Rather than feeling inferior, I gained a sense of collegiality with the other people there. I found that they were as afraid of exposing themselves to me as I was to them. Now I seek out those support groups. I have several that I wouldn't miss for anything. They replaced the old buddy networks, which were fun but didn't give me half as much as the managerial groups did.

You don't necessarily need to go to conferences for that information. There are a wide variety of resources, websites, affinity groups and periodicals available,* and you can find perspectives on specific issues merely by asking Google your question. While online research is helpful, it most likely won't lead to the personal relationships I built that were so enriching. So do consider in-person participation. If you're comfortable with yourself and where you're going, with what you don't know and what you need to know, you're apt to create an atmosphere of support for your employees. If you don't do it for yourself, do it for them.

GIVING BACK

Currently, I'm devoting a large part of my time to mentoring undergraduate and graduate students. The undergraduate students are mostly first-generation minority students and others who are interested in learning from my 50-plus years

---

* Check out https://socialworkmanager.org/journal/ and https://www.tandfonline.com/loi/wasw21 to begin getting acquainted with available sites.

of experience and life lessons.

Several years ago, my Florida resident association committed to raising scholarship money for our employees and their children. What's unique about this program is that no students are funded without a mentor, and the mentors are drawn from the residents. Our graduation success rate is over 90%, which I attribute in large part to the mandated mentoring program.

I also work with the University of St. Thomas in Houston and National Louis University in Chicago and have helped develop the Human Service Master's curricula at both these schools. The new courses of study show great promise and have the potential to become national models for human service management education. Most of the courses are taught by experienced, successful human service managers, who become adjunct faculty.

One of my most successful mentoring experiences involved Barbara, a woman who had five children. I had observed Barbara working as a cook for a number of years, and there was something about her that intrigued me. She had an uncanny ability to solve problems with an attitude and disposition that clearly made her stand out from her peers.

One day I asked Barbara if she ever considered going to college. "Not me, Mr. Pettinelli," she said, "I've got five little ones at home, and I just have no time for college." I told her that I was willing to bet that she had what it took to get her degree, would mentor her through the experience and help her financially if she was interested. We agreed that she could take one or two courses at the state university just to see how she felt about the experience.

Well, Barbara shone! Not only did she do well, but she was offered a scholarship after one semester toward the completion of her BA. My role was to be available to her as she needed me. In the beginning, we met personally or talked a couple of times a week. We talked about time management, study habits and, most important, how to avail herself of the myriad supports the university offered.

One night Barbara called me in a panic because, as much as she tried, she could not work her way through the word problems in her college math course. Now, anyone acquainted with me knows that I'm no math wizard. Thankfully, I got the help I needed in school to pass the math courses needed for graduation. Surrounding myself with people who were smarter than I was helped. Math also helped me understand basic financial and rudimentary statistical analysis skills that I used regularly to measure the qualitative and quantitative effects of our company's service delivery systems.

After finding some internet resources, I was able to help Barbara help herself through her math crisis. I stressed that if she was going to achieve any degree of skill and confidence in using her math skills, she would have to practice until those skills became second nature. I asked Barb to do three word problems a day for three weeks and correct the mistakes she had made using the internet resource we'd found. At the end of three weeks, Barb was "acing" her math tests. The point here is simple. When you acquire any new skill like tennis, golf, basketball or management, you have to practice it with feedback on your performance until the new skill becomes a natural part of you. That's why you need a mentor.

Having successfully navigated the university bureaucracy–which was no easy task–Barbara graduated in two years with a BA in Food Service Management. Her entire family attended her graduation, and she told me that her experience helped her children understand, in real-life terms, the effort and benefit of getting an education. Barbara is now working at a premiere dining club and has just been promoted to assistant manager.

So what does this story have to do with you? If you are a new manager, look to work for the best manager and mentor you can find. If you find yourself working for someone less skilled, go find yourself someone who has a better grasp of management principles to mentor you. Many successful retired and soon-to-be-retired human service managers are ready to help. Find out who the most successful service providers are in your area. You'll be surprised at how many of your colleagues will be able to name several managers, who are well-known and respected in your service community. Seek these people out and ask them to become your mentor. Remember, these managers were probably mentored themselves in some fashion that contributed to their success. Now they're ready to give back.

And if you are a seasoned, successful manager, please consider becoming a mentor to someone who needs you. We owe it to all the people who were there for us when we needed them to give back.

A SENSE OF BALANCE

The message I grew up with from my father, an Italian immigrant, was, "You don't have time to rest. You have to improve yourself; do better than I do. That's why I came to this country, by God, and you as my child are going to live the American dream. You do that by working incessantly." In my neighborhood in New York, I heard that message in Italian. In other neighborhoods, children may still hear it in Chinese, Hindi, Polish, Russian, Tagalong, Hebrew, German, Korean, English and dozens of other languages. It's the American work ethic.

Yet, in recent years, attitudes toward work have evolved

from "You should work continuously" to "You should work well." We talk about topics, such as emotional intelligence, as being crucial to successful leadership. We expect leaders to develop good relationships with employees and use methods, such as coaching, listening and positive reinforcement. So I would say, "Do the best you can, but maintain your balance."

Sometimes people talk about separating their work lives from their personal lives. The truth is, the healthiest people are fully integrated. With all my foibles and craziness, I am, I think, the same person at work as I am at home. Although I may deal with things differently, I am still consistent. The same things delight me, and the same things make me angry. If my son saw me at my office, he would recognize me as his father.

I wasn't always that way. I used to put on my work face, my home face, and this face and that face. But sometimes I forgot which face I was supposed to wear. I had this mix of faces that eventually blended together.

Your life as a manager will invade your private life in a way you'd better be ready for. It will tap you on the shoulder at times when you're not expecting it. Wherever you are, you'll find yourself thinking about your responsibilities and the shaping of your organization. Managers find that they can no longer finish work, go home and leave it all behind.

Ideas spring up during times of relaxation and demand to be processed. If you don't allow yourself creative time during the work day, you'll find that the invasion into your personal life never ends. But no matter how much time you give yourself at work, you can't turn off your mind at home. Significant others need to know that. You need to sit down and make them aware of what's happening so they're not taken by surprise. "What happened to you?" they may ask, "You weren't this way before. What's wrong?" Prepare yourself.

Sometimes, when talking about their leisure or family, people refer to "quality time." "I don't spend a lot of time," they say, "but the time I spend is quality time." Be aware that there is a level of quantity you can't go below and still have quality time. It's a way of taking care of yourself. You have to allow yourself that time. As a manager, you probably make more money than you did as a line person. You need to treat yourself, whether that means going shopping or playing your favorite sport or going on vacation. Your extra income allows you to do things you couldn't do without it. That's one of your rewards. A lot of us, especially in human services, find it difficult to say, "I'm going to be selfish now." Being "selfish" is taking care of yourself. And if you're not selfish sometimes, you can't be selfless when you need to.

I have a theory about emotional stability. I believe everybody is born with a well, and the way we develop that well over time either keeps the structure solid or causes it to crumble.

No matter how much water you pour in a well that isn't properly cared for, you never have enough. It leaks out. But if you maintain your well, not only is there plenty of water for you but there's water for everybody. You can give gallons away and always have enough left for yourself because the container is constantly replenished. Too many of us scrape bottom. We try to ladle out water for others and come up with stones. We ask, "Why is there no water down there?"

Because we didn't maintain the well.

Epilogue

I didn't want this book to be yet another academic treatise on the philosophy of management. Rather, I wanted it to be a document of my own experiences in developing a human service organization. Most of all, I wanted it to be useful. If I've learned anything in my years in management, it is that there is no right way to manage. But you have to be willing to try. You have to be willing to make the effort and take that leap of faith.

Let me re-emphasize the importance of appropriate support systems. Management is a very difficult profession. You can save yourself a lot of pain by trying out techniques on supportive people before you actually implement those techniques. A reliable support system will energize you to act regardless of any initial fear you might have of making a mistake. The support systems I had in my directors and staff enabled me to test the veracity and validity of management decisions before they became "law."

Keep in mind that you are part of a team even though you're the leader, and you're only as good as that team. It's hard to make decisions about who should play on the team and who shouldn't. It's hard to realize that somebody you thought was going to work out, isn't, and to let that person go with dignity. We all love to hire people; we hate to let them go. But the team must be your team, must fit with your personality. There are lots of capable people out there, but you won't click with all of them. You need to hear that click.

You probably have management techniques of your own that you find helpful. Share your philosophies and practices with colleagues, but do it in a format that enables them to truly benefit from your experiences. Attend seminars. Allow yourself time to sit down and talk with other managers, even though they are not in what appear to be immediately related fields. You'll be surprised at how many people are scraping, as you are, for answers.

Commit yourself now to learning the skills you need to manage your operations effectively. Practice those skills under the tutelage of a trained, successful manager (mentor) who cares about you and your professional development.

Commit to taking care of yourself. Managing is hard, and new managers especially are very vulnerable to exercising poor time management and get "burned out" in a short period of time. New managers try to do everything themselves rather than delegate to their staff because they are often petrified of failure. It's hard to let go when you don't trust your skills. Prepare yourself the best you can, take the risk and do it. Sometimes you will fail. But it is in failure that your mettle will be tested and you will learn the most. If you expect to fail at times and know that it's inevitable, you will be in a wonderful position to learn from your mistakes, profit from them and determine how not to repeat your mistakes. Sharing your failures with your mentor will provide you with non-judgmental and objective feedback.

In order to be successful, you will need to embrace your management role as one of the most important life decisions you will ever make. Reimagine yourself as a manager who is dedicated to learning new skills and constantly evaluating his or her performance. Remember, if you are going to manage others, you need to manage yourself first.

If this book has any utility at all, my hope is that it will develop a foundation for your continuous learning and skill acquisition. I hope I have challenged you to dedicate yourself to your own self-development. Like any profession, you will need to acquire an ever-evolving knowledge base coupled with supervised practice. I wish you all the best!

Certainly, I have not written the definitive work on human service management. If you are a young, emerging leader, I hope you will view this book as a vehicle to encourage the sharing of ideas, beliefs and ideals. The time is long overdue for us to feel okay about admitting what we do and don't know.

I, for one, would welcome the chance to celebrate your thoughts.

Appendix

Companies often make the mistake of setting a course for change without measuring that change. However, standardized instruments can provide the answers to vital questions about a company's performance by asking questions like "Did we move in a positive direction this year?" and "Are we providing employees with more supports or more barriers against success?"

In addition, organizational diagnostics enable managers to tune into what's going on within the company. They measure a number of elements that must be constantly monitored to ensure the company is going in the right direction.

To maintain a balance between stability and change, we at VOCA kept our eyes on our:
- Vision of the future
- Values and mission
- Organizational identity

- Interdependence between the company and our environment
- Employees' quality of work life
- Flexible, responsive organizational structure
- Effective utilization of informational technology
- Reward systems.

We developed a tool we called our "Organizational Values Questionnaire" that was distributed to all of our employees. The tool polled them on ten quality-of-work issues that plugged directly into the elements of change we found important. We wanted to be sure our employees found these issues important as well. The surveys were unsigned and confidential with space for people to make comments–and some people were not afraid to share what they thought. Here are the ten factors:

1. Input: This measured how employees perceived their ability to have input into how their jobs were performed. Scores went up when we introduced the idea of teamwork.

2. Freedom: This measured job autonomy. Initially, we found that people felt they needed to consult supervisors on every question and that if they made wrong decisions, they might be fired. We gave people more freedom, believing that if people made mistakes and had the opportunity to process them, they'd have a better sense of how to handle situations in the future.

3. Personal Control: This combination of Input and freedom measured people's perceptions of whether they could exercise control without fear of what might happen in the future.

4. Challenging: We wanted jobs to be challenging, but not so challenging that people would be stressed out.

5. Solution Oriented: We wanted to solve problems without getting sidetracked or creating new ones.

6. Variety in Job: We increased our score here when we moved from very specific job descriptions to more cross-functional tasks and work done by teams.

7. MIS (Management Information Systems) Adequate: Getting information to where it needed to be had been a problem for us. We wanted to chart any improvement.

8. Walk the Talk: Our first survey said we talked about how great VOCA was, but there was a gap between talk and action. When we started doing what we said we would, employees trusted more and were better able to communicate honestly without fear of retribution.

9. Commitment: We sometimes forgot to nurture our people. When we remembered, people felt more empowered with an increased sense of belonging, alignment and family.

10. **Work Environment:** This was our highest ranking category. Employees believed that we had high standards, what we did had value, they were valued, our people were friendly and our facilities were comfortable. They felt we were more like a home than a factory.

Today, there are numerous options for online surveys that measure these and similar factors. You might want to look at an existing survey package or, as we did, create your own in keeping with your standards.

Bibliography

Acuff, Jerry, with Wally Wood. *The Relationship Edge in Business: Connecting with Customers and Colleagues When It Counts.* Hoboken, NJ: John Wiley & Sons, 2004.

Albrecht, Karl, and Ron Zemke. *Service America! Doing Business in the New Economy.* New York: Warner Books, 1990.

Bacon, Terry R. *What People Want: A Manager's Guide to Building Trust-Based Relationships with Your People.* Mountain View, CA: Davies-Black, 2006.

Band, W.A. *Creating Value for Customers: Designing and Implementing a Total Corporate Strategy.* New York: John Wiley & Sons, 1991.

Blazek, Jody. *Nonprofit Financial Planning Made Easy.* Hoboken, NJ: John Wiley & Sons, 2008.

Carlson, Mim, and Margaret Donohoe. *The Executive*

Director's Guide to Thriving as a Nonprofit (2nd ed.) San Francisco, CA: Jossey-Bass, 2010.

Collins, James C., and Jerry I. Porras. *Built to Last: Successful Habits of Visionary Companies*. New York: HarperCollins, 2004.

Coyle, Daniel. *The Culture Code: The Secrets of Highly Successful Groups*. New York: Bantam Books, 2018.

Daniels, Aubrey C. *Bringing Out the Best in People: How to Apply the Astonishing Power of Positive Reinforcement* (3rd ed.) New York: McGraw-Hill Education, 2016.

_____. *Measure of a Leader: The Legendary Leadership Formula for Producing Exceptional Performers and Outstanding Results*. New York: McGraw-Hill, 2007.

_____. *Oops! 13 Management Practices That Waste Time and Money (and what to do instead)*. Atlanta, GA: Performance Management Publications, 2009.

Dobyns, Lloyd, and Clare Crawford-Mason. *Quality or Else: The Revolution in World Business*. Boston, MA: Houghton Mifflin, 1993.

Drucker, Peter F. *Managing for the Future: The 1990s and Beyond*. New York: Truman Talley Books/Dutton, 1991.

_____. *Managing the Non-Profit Organization: Principles and Practices.* New York: HarperCollins, 1990.

Dykstra, Art. *Outcome Management: Achieving Outcomes for People with Disabilities.* Homewood, IL: High Tide Press, 1995.

Elliott, Glenn, and Debra Corey. *Build It: The Rebel Playbook for World-Class Employee Engagement.* Chichester, West Sussex, UK: John Wiley & Sons, 2018.

Evenson, Renee. *Customer Service Training 101: Quick and Easy Techniques That Get Great Results.* New York: AMACOM, 2018.

Frei, Frances, and Anne Morriss. *Uncommon Service: How to Win by Putting Customers at the Core of Your Business.* Boston, MA: Harvard Business Review Press, 2012.

Goulston, Mark. *Just Listen: Discover the Secret to Getting Through to Absolutely Anyone.* New York: AMACOM, 2010.

Grensing-Pophal, Lin. *Employee Management for Small Business.* Bellingham, WA: Self-Counsel Press, 2005.

Hanberg, Erik. *The Little Book of Gold: Fundraising for Small (and Very Small) Nonprofits.* Tacoma, WA: Side x Side Publishing, 2011.

Juran, J.M. *Juran on Quality by Design: The New Steps for Planning Quality into Goods and Services.* New York: The Free Press, 1992.

_____. *Juran on Leadership for Quality: An Executive Handbook.* New York, NY: The Free Press, 1989.

Kaufman, Ron. *Uplifting Service: The Proven Path to Delighting Your Customers, Colleagues, and Everyone Else You Meet.* Ashland, OH: Evolve Publishing, 2012.

Nelson-Walker, Roberta. *Fund Raising for Social Service Agencies.* Homewood, IL: High Tide Press, 2005.

Patterson, Kerry et al. *Crucial Conversations: Tools for Talking When the Stakes Are High* (2nd ed.). New York: McGraw-Hill, 2012.

Rock, David. *Quiet Leadership: Six Steps to Transforming Performance at Work.* New York: Collins, 2006.

Stanier, Michael Bungay. *The Coaching Habit: Say Less, Ask More & Change the Way You Lead Forever.* Toronto, ON: Box of Crayons Press, 2016.

Steckel, Richard. *Cold Cash for Warm Hearts: 101 Best Social Marketing Initiatives.* Homewood, IL: High Tide Press, 2004.

About
the Author

Vincent D. Pettinelli, MSW, has over 50 years of senior management experience in the organization, administration, and provision of services to persons with intellectual and developmental disabilities, mental illness and geriatric dementia in both the public and private sectors.

He began his career in government administration, serving as Director of Education for the Mental Health Association of Houston/Harris County, Texas; Director of Regional Services for the South Carolina Department of Mental Retardation; Commissioner for Mental Retardation for the Pennsylvania State Department of Public Welfare; and Director of the State of Ohio Joint Mental Health and Mental Retardation Advisory Review Commission.

In 1979, after 15 years as a top management executive in government, Vince founded PeopleServe, Inc. as one of the first of its kind for-profit company, created to serve persons with significant disabilities. PeopleServe was acquired by

ResCare, Inc., in June of 1999.

An author, lecturer and educator, Vince has authored articles and presented conference papers for such distinguished groups as the AAIDD and the American Psychotherapy Association, among others. In 2010, Vince was selected as a contributor to the book *How They Did It* by Robert Jordan. This book details the accomplishments of successful entrepreneurs in the Midwest.

Vince received his BA degree from the University of St. Thomas (Houston, TX), and his MSW from Tulane University (New Orleans, LA). In addition, he completed post-graduate study at the University of Alabama and the University of Wisconsin. As an educator, Vince has served on the adjunct faculty of the Ohio State University School of Social Work, the University of South Carolina Department of Social Work, and the Temple University School of Social Work.

At present, Vince spends much of his time mentoring graduate and undergraduate students. He counts it a privilege to offer them invaluable wisdom, support and guidance drawn from his years of experience as an entrepreneur and a manager.